LANDHÄUSER
IN HOLLAND

COUNTRY HOUSES
OF HOLLAND

LES MAISONS
ROMANTIQUES
DE HOLLANDE

LANDHÄUSER IN HOLLAND

COUNTRY HOUSES OF HOLLAND

LES MAISONS ROMANTIQUES DE HOLLANDE

Barbara & René Stoeltie

EDITED BY · HERAUSGEGEBEN VON · SOUS LA DIRECTION DE
Angelika Taschen

TASCHEN

KÖLN LONDON MADRID NEW YORK PARIS TOKYO

ROMANTISCHE LANDHÄUSER IN *Holland*

Carel Fabritius, *Der Distelfink · The Goldfinch · Le Chardonneret* (1654), Mauritshuis, Den Haag

OBEN · ABOVE · CI-DESSUS: Jan Vermeer, *Ansicht von Delft · View of Delft · Vue de Delft* (um 1660–1661), Detail, Mauritshuis, Den Haag

»Holland« lässt sofort an ganz bestimmte Bilder denken: Windmühlen, deren Flügel sich unter einem wolkenschweren Himmel drehen, eine Herde schwarz-weißer Kühe, die auf einer scheinbar grenzenlosen Weide grast, den rauen Nordwind, der unerbittlich über Tulpenfelder fegt, oder auch die dunklen Silhouetten einiger Schlittschuhläufer, die sich abzeichnen am verschneiten Horizont, der nur manchmal von den Umrissen einer kleinen Kirche, eines einsamen Baumes oder eines reetgedeckten Bauernhauses unterbrochen wird.

Unsere Assoziationen werden auch heute noch geprägt von Rembrandt, Pieter de Hooch, Vermeer, Jacob van Ruisdael oder Meindert Hobbema, die holländische Landschaften und Interieurs in ihren Gemälden verewigt haben. Sie haben uns das typische Erscheinungsbild dieses flachen Landes nahe gebracht: die vielen langen Alleen, gesäumt von schmalen Bäumen, die der Westwind gekrümmt hat; das beeindruckende Netz von Kanälen und Flüssen, in denen sich die zahllosen Wolken und ein schmales Stück blauer Himmel spiegeln; und schließlich die Vielzahl der unterschiedlichsten Häuser – von ganz vornehm bis ganz schlicht. Hier entdeckt man glänzende Marmorböden, blitzblank poliertes Kupfer, erfreut sich an einem schönen Blumenstrauß, genießt den kühlen Rhein-

ROMANTIC COUNTRY HOUSES OF *Holland*

You need only utter the word "Holland" to conjure up a host of stereotyped images. You will think, perhaps, of windmills slowly turning under clouded blue skies, or herds of black and white Friesian cows grazing in meadows that stretch into the middle distance. And more: pitiless winds out of the north lashing fields of tulips, muffled silhouettes of skaters against the snow, and winter landscapes whose relentless sameness is broken only by the occasional church spire, solitary tree, or thatched farmhouse.

Inevitably our idea of Holland is influenced by the landscapes and interiors of Rembrandt, Pieter de Hooch, Vermeer, Jacob van Ruisdael or Meindert Hobbema. These taught us that the Low Countries also have their slender trees bent sideways by the winds, their cloud-reflecting canals and rivers, and above all the snug houses of all degrees of people. In these houses we expect to find rich gleaming marble floors, polished coppers, pretty bouquets of flowers, pitchers brimming with hock, and pewter dishes laden with oysters – proof, if proof were needed, that Calvin and Epicurus are perfectly reconciled in the souls of the Dutch.

The Dutch people love their houses and are fiercely proud of their possessions. Here are no locked shutters or drawn cur-

Clara Peeters, *Käse mit Mandeln und Bretzeln · Cheeses with Almonds and Pretzels · Fromage avec amandes et bretzels* (um 1612–1615), The Richard Green Gallery, London

LES MAISONS ROMANTIQUES DE *Hollande*

Nous entendons le mot «Hollande» et aussitôt notre esprit se remplit d'images stéréotypes: un moulin à vent tourne ses ailes sous un ciel lourd de nuages, un troupeau de vaches blanches tachées de noir broutent l'herbe dans une prairie qui semble s'étendre à perte de vue, un vent du Nord impitoyable fouette un champ où poussent des rangées interminables de tulipes, et les silhouettes sombres de quelques patineurs emmitouflés se dessinent sur un fond de paysage enneigé interrompu ci et là par les contours d'une petite église, d'un arbre solitaire et d'une maison de campagne à toit de chaume.

Il est inévitable que le souvenir de la Hollande soit étroitement lié aux paysages et aux intérieurs immortalisés par Rembrandt, Pieter de Hooch, Vermeer, Jacob van Ruisdael ou Meindert Hobbema. Ces peintres nous ont appris que ce plat pays est peuplé de longues allées bordées d'arbres sveltes, courbés par la force des zéphyrs, d'un réseau impressionnant de canaux et de rivières où se reflètent des masses de nuages et un maigre pan de ciel bleu et d'une multitude de maisons, de la plus noble à la plus humble, dans lesquelles on découvre la richesse d'un sol en marbre luisant de propreté et des cuivres rageusement astiqués. La présence d'un joli bouquet de fleurs, d'un pichet de vin du Rhin écumant et d'un plat en étain surchargé d'huîtres, trahissent un mariage heureux entre le calvinisme et l'épicurisme.

Les Hollandais entretiennent leur maison avec amour et se

Meindert Hobbema,
*Die Allee von Middel-
harnis · Avenue at
Middelharnis · L'Allée
de Middelharnis*
(1689), Detail, Na-
tional Gallery, London

wein aus dem Krug und die dazu auf einer Zinnplatte servierten Austern – ein wunderbares Zusammenspiel von kalvinistischer Bescheidenheit und Luxus.

Die Holländer pflegen ihre Häuser und sind stolz auf ihren Besitz. Hier gibt es kaum geschlossene Fensterläden oder zugezogene Vorhänge. In der Stadt ebenso wie auf dem Land gestatten große Fenster einen indiskreten Blick in ein Zimmer mit einem großen Eichentisch, auf die Ahnengalerie oder die einfache Topfgeranie. Der Anblick ist so verlockend, dass man am liebsten die angelehnte Tür öffnen und den nach guter Seife duftenden Raum betreten möchte. Man möchte sich in einen der tiefen Sessel am Kamin mit den Delfter Kacheln sinken lassen und dem monotonen Ticken der Nussbaumuhr lauschen, das den Raum mit Frieden und Ruhe erfüllt.

Und natürlich gibt es die berühmten Käsesorten, die strohfarbene Butter, die cremige Milch, die salzigen Heringe, die man genüsslich auf der Straße isst, den klaren Genever, der die Zunge lockert und – um mit Jacques Brels Worten zu sprechen – »diesen Himmel, der so tief hängt, dass der Kanal daran klebt«. Aber es existiert auch das andere, das wenig bekannte Holland im Verborgenen, das seine mit Schätzen gefüllten Schlösser gern vor neugierigen Blicken schützt und mit Hecken und kirchturmhohen Bäumen die Höfe abschirmt, in denen die Zeit stehen geblieben ist. Hier leben Künstler und liebenswerte Exzentriker in einer Welt, die weit entfernt scheint von dem hektischen Leben unserer Zeit. Dieses Holland gilt es noch zu entdecken, begeben Sie sich mit uns auf die Suche!

tains; in both town and country windows are deliberately left unveiled so you can see straight into rooms where the big oak tables, portraits of ancestors, and flower pots bursting with geraniums make you want to push the half open door and go in. And when you do, there will be a scent of fresh soap and a deep chair to sit in by the fireplace, with its Delft tiles, while the walnut-veneered grandfather clock ticks away, filling the room with a sense of quiet and serenity.

Of course there are the famous cheeses, the straw-yellow butter, the creamy milk, the pickled herrings you eat standing in the street; also "genever", the syrupy Dutch gin, which oils the tongue, and the sky described by Jacques Brel as "… so low the canals are hung on it". Yet there's another Holland, hidden this time, a Holland which likes to spread out the treasures of its castles before the eyes of the curious, a Holland of farms surrounded by tall hedges and trees where time seems to have stopped and where artists and eccentrics are carefully shielded against the onset of the helter-skelter outside world. This is the Holland we have sought to describe in this book.

Salomon van Ruysdael, *Überfahrt bei Nimwegen · The Crossing at Nimwegen · Le Bac près de Nimègues* (1647), Detail, Rheinisches Landesmuseum, Bonn

montrent fiers de leurs possessions. Ici point de volets fermés ni de rideaux tirés mais, à la ville comme à la campagne, de grandes fenêtres dénuées de rideaux qui vous offrent le spectacle indiscret d'une pièce où trônent une grande table en chêne, quelques portraits d'ancêtres ou un simple géranium en pot. Vous avez alors envie de pousser la porte entrebâillée, d'entrer dans cette demeure qui fleure bon le savon et de vous asseoir dans un fauteuil profond près de la cheminée entourée de carreaux en Delft. La grande horloge en loupe de noyer au tic-tac monotone crée une ambiance paisible et calme.

La Hollande, ce sont bien sûr ces fromages célèbres, ce beurre couleur de paille, ce lait onctueux, ces harengs crus que l'on déguste dans la rue à belles dents, ce genièvre sirupeux qui délie les langues et, pour parler avec Jacques Brel, «ce ciel si bas qu'un canal s'est pendu». Mais il en existe une autre, peu connue et cachottière, qui aime dissimuler ses châteaux bourrés de trésors à l'œil investigateur des curieux, qui dresse des frontières de haies et d'arbres hauts comme des cathédrales autour des fermes où le temps semble s'être arrêté et qui protège le fruit de l'imagination d'un artiste ou la douce folie d'un excentrique contre les agressions d'une vie quotidienne au rythme de plus en plus effréné. Cette Hollande là reste à explorer … Partons à la découverte!

Pieter de Hooch, *Soldaten und Frau beim Trinken im Hof · Two Soldiers and a Woman Drinking in a Courtyard · Deux Soldats et une femme buvant dans une cour* (um 1658–1660), Detail, National Gallery of Art, Washington, D.C., Andrew Mellon Collection

EEN VISSERSHAVEN

Noord-Holland

Der Fischerhafen von Volendam, im Norden von Amsterdam gegenüber vom Zuiderzee, ist seltsamerweise dank des Touristenstroms gut erhalten. Zahllose Besucher aus aller Welt sind begeistert von der quirligen Atmosphäre, den historischen Kostümen, den niedrigen kleinen Häuschen, die an Puppenhäuser erinnern, und den köstlichen Fischgerichten, bei denen sich vor allem roher Hering und geräucherter Meeraal besonderer Beliebtheit erfreuen. Schlendert man durch die engen Gassen und den Hafen, wo rege Betriebsamkeit herrscht, gesellen sich einige Neugierige allmählich zu der Menschenmenge, die sich um die Marktstände schart, und warten auf die Ankunft der Boote mit prall gefüllten Fangnetzen voll silbrig glänzender Fische. Darunter befinden sich auch ein paar Einwohner in Trachten, die Mützen und derbe schwarze Wollhosen tragen oder sich mit Spitzenhauben und einem korallenroten Halsband mit schwerem Goldverschluß schmücken. Sehnsucht nach der Vergangenheit? Sicherlich. Aber auch der tief verwurzelte Respekt vor dem historischen Erbe, der sich in der sorgsamen Erhaltung eines Fischerhauses mit apfelblüten-roten Vertäfelungen ausdrückt, das noch immer den Geruch von anno dazumal verströmt.

VORHERGEHENDE DOPPELSEITE: *Auf einem der Wellenbrecher warten zahlreiche Rundhölzer darauf, zu einem Landesteg verarbeitet zu werden.*
LINKS: *Der bekannte Volksheld »Pul« steht in einer Tracht, wie man sie einst in den Sommermonaten trug, auf einem der Boote.*

PREVIOUS PAGES: *wooden poles on one of the breakwaters, waiting to be turned into a new landing stage.*
LEFT: *"Pul", a popular local character, standing on one of the fishing boats in traditional local costume. This version was worn in summer.*

DOUBLE PAGE PRÉCÉDENTE: *Sur un des brise-lames, les rondins entassés attendent d'être transformés en appontement.*
A GAUCHE: *Dans une embarcation, «Pul», un personnage populaire, porte le costume traditionnel que l'on arborait jadis pendant les mois d'été.*

The fishing port of Volendam, on the Zuiderzee to the north of Amsterdam, has survived – strangely enough – thanks to a steady influx of tourists from all over the world. They come in large numbers to soak up the town's lively atmosphere, to see its traditional costumes and small low buildings decorated like doll's houses, and to consume the succulent fish (raw herring, smoked eel) for which Volendam is justly famous. Visitors walking in the narrow streets and in the busy harbour area are irresistibly drawn to the quayside, where a throng awaits the arrival of the boats and their silvery fish. The crowd will always include one or two people wearing traditional costumes – bonnets and baggy black worsted trousers, pleated lace caps and red coral collars with gold clasps. Nostalgia for the past? Very much so. But the visitors also come out of respect for the town's cultural heritage, as reflected in the careful preservation of a humble fisherman's house with its original apple-blossom pink panelling.

Hinter dem Fischmarkt füllen die Fischer die Meeraale in Reusen um – die letzte Station vor der Räucherkammer.

Behind the market stall, fishermen dump sea eels out of their nets before sending them on to the smoke-house.

Derrière la poissonnerie, les pêcheurs transvasent les anguilles dans des nasses, leur ultime refuge avant de passer au fumoir.

Le port de pêche de Volendam est situé au nord d'Amsterdam et fait face au Zuiderzee. Etrangement, ce sont les touristes venus du monde entier qui l'ont préservé: ils viennent en grand nombre s'imprégner de son ambiance animée, admirer les costumes traditionnels et les petites maisons basses, décorées comme des maisons de poupée, et savourer les poissons succulents parmi lesquels le hareng cru et l'anguille fumée ont une place d'honneur. En se promenant dans les rues étroites et sur le port qui grouille d'une activité fiévreuse, les curieux se laissent bercer doucement au rythme d'une foule qui s'empresse autour des étaux du marché et qui guette l'arrivée des bateaux et de leurs filets gonflés par des masses scintillantes de poissons argentés. Ils désignent du doigt les rares habitants en costume traditionnel, accoutrés d'un bonnet et d'un pantalon bouffant en grosse laine noire ou d'une coiffe en dentelle plissée et d'un «collier de chien» en corail rouge orné d'un lourd fermoir en or. Nostalgie du passé? Certes. Mais aussi: un respect profond pour le patrimoine culturel qui se reflète dans la préservation jalouse d'une maison de pêcheur aux lambris «rouge fleur de pommier» où flotte toujours le parfum d'antan.

Die Afra Maria ist wieder in den Hafen eingelaufen und einer der Reiher wartet bereits ungeduldig auf seinen Anteil der Beute.

The Afra Maria is back in port: a heron waits for a share of her catch.

Le Afra Maria est rentré au port et un des hérons attend sa part avec impatience.

LINKE SEITE: *In diesem mit nostalgischen Bildern und Statuen reich geschmückten Interieur – Volendam ist seit jeher katholisch – genießt Liesbeth Woestenburg in Original-Tracht eine Tasse Tee.*

RECHTS: *Auf einem Delfter Porzellanteller aus dem 17. Jahrhundert warten die geräucherten Fische, Sprotten und Makrele, darauf, zu köstlichen Filets verarbeitet zu werden. Die Meeresaale daneben sind eine typisch holländische Spezialität.*

FACING PAGE: *In this old-fashioned interior, filled with religious images and statuettes (Volendam has always been a Catholic community) Liesbeth Woestenburg, an authentic Volendammer, takes tea in her traditional costume.*

RIGHT: *On a 17th-century Delft dish, smoked sprats and a smoked mackerel wait to be filleted; likewise a couple of smoked eels, a Dutch speciality.*

PAGE DE GAUCHE: *Dans cet intérieur vieillot, bourré d'images et de statuettes pieuses – Volendam a toujours été une commune catholique –, Liesbeth Woestenburg prend le thé en costume traditionnel.*

A DROITE: *Sur un plat en Delft 17ᵉ, les sprats et le maquereau fumés attendent d'être réduits en filets savoureux. A droite, des anguilles fumées – une spécialité hollandaise – subiront le même sort.*

Wie durch ein Wunder wurden die Innen-räume der Familie Snoek (Hecht!) in der Vissersstraat (Fischer-strasse!) vor der Zer-störung durch die »Ver-eniging Oud Volen-dam« bewahrt. Möbel, Wände im Farbton »appelbloesem« (Apfel-blüte), Kupferwaren und der mit Tuch aus-gelegte Boden stammen vom Anfang des 19. Jahrhunderts.

Miraculously, the inte-rior of the Snoek family (Snoek means "pike" in Dutch) was saved from demolition by the "Ver-eniging Oud Volen-dam". The furniture, the colours on the walls – called appelbloesem – the coppers, and the floor with its tarpaulin covering, all date from the beginning of the 19th century.

L'intérieur de la famille Snoek (brochet!) dans la Vissersstraat (la rue des pêcheurs!) a été sauvé de la démolition par la «Vereniging Oud Volen-dam». Le mobilier, les murs couleur «appel-bloesem», fleur de pom-mier, les cuivres et le sol couvert de toile de bâche datent du début du 19e siècle.

LINKS: »*Komt allen tot Mij*« – *Kommt alle zu mir* – *grüßt ein mehrfarbiger Christus aus Gips umgeben von Engeln und künstlichen Blumen die Gläubigen.*

LEFT: *"Komt allen tot Mij": "Come unto me (all ye who are heavy laden)": A beckoning Christ made of painted plaster, surrounded by angels and artificial flowers.*

A GAUCHE: «*Komt allen tot Mij*» – *Venez Tous Vers Moi* – *un Christ en plâtre polychrome, entouré d'anges et de fleurs artificielles, fait signe aux croyants.*

FACING PAGE: *It's hard to believe this alcove once accommodated as many as five people: father, mother and youngest in the top crib, and two more offspring in the bottom one.*

RIGHT: *on a round-bellied chest of drawers, glass-covered statuettes of Joseph, Mary and Christ on the Cross.*

LINKE SEITE: *Schwer vorstellbar, daß dieser Alkoven einst fünf Personen beherbergte – den Vater, die Mutter und den letztgeborenen, mitsamt zwei Kindern in der »kribbe« darunter!*

RECHTS: *Auf der gewölbten Kommode werden der heilige Joseph, der heilige Jungfrau und ein »Christus am Kreuz« durch Glaskuppeln vor Staub geschützt.*

PAGE DE GAUCHE: *On a peine à croire que l'alcôve abritait cinq personnes – le père, la mère et le dernier né dans la partie supérieure, et deux enfant dans la «kribbe» en dessous.*

A DROITE: *Sur la commode bombée, des globes en verre protègent de la poussière les statuettes de saint Joseph, de la sainte Vierge et une Crucifixion.*

Czaar Peterhuisje

Noord-Holland

Die Sonne war an diesem Sonntag im August 1697 gerade aufgegangen, als der Hufschmied Gerrit Kist, ein leidenschaftlicher Angler, auf dem Fluss Zaan die hohe Gestalt seines ehemaligen »Herrn«, Peter des Großen von Russland, auf einer Barke vorbeiziehen sah! Als der Zar ihm befahl, seine Identität geheim zu halten und ihm Kost und Logis zu geben, nahm ihn Kist in seiner kleinen Hütte in Zaandam auf, verjagte die Witwe, die das Hinterhaus bewohnte und brachte ihn in zwei engen Zimmern unter. Diese waren nur mit einem Alkovenbett, einem Ofen, einem Tisch und zwei Stühlen eingerichtet. Peter der Große war inkognito nach Holland gekommen, um sich mit der Schiffsbautechnik vertraut zu machen und arbeitete als Schreiner in der Werft von Lijns Rogge in Zaandam. Sein Pseudonym lautete »Pjotr Michajlow«, aber binnen einer Woche wurde er erkannt und musste nach Amsterdam fliehen und schließlich Holland verlassen. Nach seinem Tod wurde die Hütte zu einer Besuchsstätte von so großer Beliebtheit, dass man beschloss, das Quartier des Zaren zu erhalten. König Wilhelm III. der Niederlande schenkte es den Romanoffs und Zar Nikolaus II. ließ es 1895 von dem Architekten Salm in ein Gebäude aus Stein »einbauen«. Seitdem kommen Besucher aus aller Welt, um die karge Unterkunft des Mannes zu bestaunen, der sich als Pjotr Michajlow ausgab …

On an early August morning in 1697, a blacksmith by the name of Gerrit Kist was fishing on the banks of the River Zaan. All of a sudden a boat came up, and in it he recognised the tall figure of his former overlord, Tsar Peter the Great of Russia. The Tsar announced that he needed lodgings in the vicinity, but wished his identity to remain a secret. Gerrit immediately led him to his own cabin at Zaandam, expelled the widow who occupied the back of the house and placed her two vacated rooms at the Tsar's disposal. Peter the Great had come to Holland incognito to spy out the techniques of Dutch naval construction. He took a carpenter's job at the shipyards of Lijns Rogge at Zaandam under the pseudonym of Pjotr Michajlow, but after a week the population discovered his identity and he was obliged to return to Amsterdam and quit Holland. After his death, the cabin was turned into a museum. It was subsequently given to the Romanovs by William III of the Netherlands and in 1895 Tsar Nicolas II had it embalmed in a stone building by the architect Salm. Since then it has received a steady procession of visitors from all over the planet, who come to marvel at the modest lodgings of the monarch who went by the name of Pjotr Michajlow.

Le soleil vient de se lever ce dimanche d'août de l'année 1697 lorsque le maréchal-ferrant Gerrit Kist, un fervent pêcheur, voit passer une barque sur la rivière Zaan, dans laquelle il reconnaît la haute stature de son ancien «patron», Pierre le Grand, tsar de Russie! Quand celui-ci lui ordonne de ne pas révéler son identité et de lui offrir le gîte et le couvert, Kist se voit contraint de l'amener dans son humble cabanon à Zaandam, de chasser la veuve qui occupe les pièces de l'arrière et de l'héberger dans ces deux pièces exiguës uniquement équipées d'un lit d'alcôve et d'un poêle et où il y a tout juste de la place pour une table et deux chaises. Pierre le Grand est venu en Hollande incognito pour s'emparer des techniques de construction navale. Pour ce faire, il s'est engagé comme menuisier sur le chantier naval de Lijns Rogge à Zaandam sous le pseudonyme de Pjotr Michajlow. Au bout d'une semaine, la population découvre son identité et il est obligé de s'enfuir à Amsterdam et de quitter la Hollande. Après sa mort, le cabanon devenu «musée» connaît une si grande popularité que l'on décide de préserver les quartiers du Tsar. Le roi Guillaume III des Pays-Bas l'offre aux Romanov, et le Tsar Nicolas II le fait «encapsuler» en 1895 par l'architecte Salm dans un bâtiment en pierre. Depuis, des visiteurs venus du monde entier viennent s'étonner du modeste logis de celui qui se fit nommer Pjotr Michajlow ...

LINKS: *An diesem robusten Esstisch aus Eiche konnte der Schreinerlehrling Pjotr Michajlow – hier als winzige Bronzestatue – seine Pläne und Manuskripte studieren.*
FOLGENDE DOPPEL-SEITE LINKS: *Jan Vermeer, Briefleserin am offenen Fenster (um 1657): Liebes- oder Abschiedsbrief? Die Antwort werden wir nie erfahren …*
FOLGENDE DOPPEL-SEITE RECHTS: *Seit fast drei Jahrhunderten kommen Besucher aus aller Welt in das kleine Zarenhaus. Einige haben sogar ihren Namen in die Fensterscheibe geritzt.*

LEFT: *On this oak refectory table, the apprentice carpenter Pjotr Michajlow studied his plans and manuscripts. The tiny bronze statue is a likeness of him.*

FOLLOWING PAGES LEFT: *Jan Vermeer, Girl Reading a Letter at an Open Window (c. 1657): Is this a love letter or a farewell note? No-one will ever know.*
FOLLOWING PAGES RIGHT: *For three centuries past, visitors have come from all over the world to Czaar Peterhuisje. Some even left their names scratched on the window panes.*

A GAUCHE: *Sur cette robuste table de réfectoire en chêne, l'apprenti menuisier Pjotr Michajlow – représenté ici par une minuscule statue en bronze – pouvait étudier ses plans et ses manuscrits.*
DOUBLE PAGE SUIVANTE A GAUCHE: *Jan Vermeer, Jeune femme lisant une lettre (vers 1657): lettre d'amour ou de rupture? Nul ne le saura jamais.*

DOUBLE PAGE SUIVANTE A DROITE: *Depuis près de trois siècles, des visiteurs du monde entier viennent se recueillir dans la modeste maison du Tsar. Certains d'entre eux ont même gravé leur nom sur les vitres de sa fenêtre.*

FACING PAGE: *The living room – which also served as a bedroom – leads through to the Tsar's study.*
RIGHT: *A wooden chair which once belonged to the Emperor stands beneath twin portraits of the Tsar and Tsarina.*

LINKE SEITE: *Der Wohnraum, der gleichzeitig als Schlafzimmer dient, führt auch in das Arbeitszimmer des Zaren.*
RECHTS: *Unter den Porträts des Zaren und der Zarin steht ein Stuhl aus gedrechseltem Holz, der dem Herrscher Russlands gehörte.*

PAGE DE GAUCHE: *Le séjour qui sert en même temps de chambre à coucher donne accès à la pièce où le Tsar travaillait.*
A DROITE: *Sous les portraits du Tsar et de la Tsarine, on a placé une chaise en bois tourné qui a appartenu à l'Empereur de Russie.*

MUSEUM BETJE WOLFF

Noord-Holland

»Hier sind meine Karten, meine Stiche, meine Bücher.
Hier gibt es die schönste Aussicht, die man sich vorstellen kann.
Hier muss ich keine meiner verstreuten Notizen,
kein verloren gegangenes Gedicht, kein Buch suchen.
Alles, was ich brauche, habe ich in meinem Kabinett hier oben,
in dem ich alle meine Tage verbringe.
Es gibt keinen Ort, der mir ebenso gefallen könnte;
und der noch dazu von einem solchen Garten umgeben wäre,
der meine Gedanken aufheitert ...«

In der Beschreibung ihres Arbeitsraums – liebevoll »Hühnerstall« genannt – unter dem Dach ihres Hauses in Middenbeemster schwärmt die Schriftstellerin Betje Wolff von dessen behaglicher Atmosphäre. Die begabte Rebellin Wolff übte vehemente Kritik an den so genannten guten Sitten und dem engstirnigen Klerus. Nach dem Tod ihres Mannes, des Pastors Adriaan Wolff, verließ Betje Wolff 1777 ihr Haus, um mit der Kollegin Agatha »Aagje« Deken zusammenzuleben, mit der sie sehr erfolgreiche Romane verfasste. Im Jahr 1950 wurde das Haus in ein Museum verwandelt. Und seitdem ist jeder, der die Ansicht des Dichters Jacobus Bellamy teilt »Wolff, das ist der Essig und Deken das Öl. Zusammen ergibt das eine köstliche Vinaigrette«, begeistert von den sensibel wiederhergerichteten Räumen.

Die Tafel eines Paravents aus dem 18. Jahrhundert zeigt eine idealisierte Dorfszene.

On one of the panels of an 18th-century screen, an idealised scene of village life.

Sur un des panneaux d'un paravent 18ᵉ, on aperçoit une scène idéalisée de la vie au village.

Die Rückansicht des Hauses mit dem Obstgarten.

View of the rear of the house from the garden, which is planted with fruit trees.

La face arrière de la maison vue du verger.

"Here are my maps, my engravings, my books
Here is the loveliest view imaginable
No need to hunt for stray drawings, poems or volumes.
This is my retreat: it has everything I want
And this is where I spend my days.
No other place pleases me as well,
Nowhere else is there a garden with such power
To brighten my thoughts …"

Describing her study – which she called "the hen house" – in the attic of her home at Middenbeemster, the writer Betje Wolff went into ecstasies over its snugness and tranquillity. A scandalous, prodigally-gifted rebel, Wolff left her home in 1777 after the death of her husband, the pastor Adriaan Wolff. Thereafter she collaborated with her fellow-writer Agatha "Aagje" Deken to produce a series of highly successful novels. In 1950, the house became a museum; and since that time those who share the view of the poet Jacobus Bellamy ("Wolff was the vinegar and Deken the oil: together they made an excellent dressing") have been able to enjoy these cunningly reconstructed interiors, and to imagine that Betje is still upstairs in her "hen house".

« Voici mes cartes, mes gravures, mes livres.
Voici la plus belle vue que l'on puisse rêver.
Je n'ai plus besoin de chercher
mes croquis dispersés, un poème égaré, un livre.
J'ai tout ce que dont j'ai besoin dans mon repère,
car c'est là haut que je passe toutes mes journées.
Il n'y a point d'endroit qui puisse autant me plaire;
et qui soit entouré d'un jardin qui égaye mes pensées …»

En décrivant son cabinet de travail – surnommé «Le Poulailler» – sous les combles de sa maison à Middenbeemster, l'écrivain Betje Wolff s'extasiait sur l'ambiance douillette et tranquille qui y régnait. Rebelle et scandaleuse, avec du talent à revendre, elle dénonça avec véhémence «les bonnes mœurs» et le clergé inflexible de son époque. Wolff quitta sa maison en 1777, après le décès de son époux, le pasteur Adriaan Wolff pour se lier d'amitié avec sa collègue Agatha «Aagje» Deken, avec laquelle elle écrivit des romans à grand succès. En 1950, la maison fut transformée en musée. Et depuis, tous ceux qui sont de l'avis du poète Jacobus Bellamy – «Wolff, c'est le vinaigre et Deken, l'huile. Ensemble cela fait une bonne vinaigrette», – peuvent dévorer des yeux un intérieur subtilement reconstruit et s'imaginer que Betje n'a jamais quitté son «Poulailler».

Vor der Einfahrt des Hauses scheint ein altes »sjeesje« auf die Ankunft der temperamentvollen Betje zu warten.

In front of the coach entrance, a period "sjeesje" awaits Betje's arrival.

Devant l'entrée cochère de la maison, un «sjeesje» d'époque semble attendre l'arrivée de la pétillante Betje.

LINKE SEITE: *Der Geschirrschrank in der Küche ist mit einem holländischen Fayence-Service aus dem 18. Jahrhundert gefüllt.*
RECHTS: *Zwar saß die Frau des Pastors Wolff nie in diesem Korbstuhl, aber die Küche ist nahezu unverändert.*

FACING PAGE: *An 18th-century Dutch earthenware dinner service fills the kitchen dresser.*
RIGHT: *Though Pastor Wolff's wife never sat in this particular wicker chair, the kitchen is otherwise the same as it was in her time.*

PAGE DE GAUCHE: *Dans le vaisselier de la cuisine, un service en faïence 18ᵉ hollandais prend toute la place.*
A DROITE: *Bien que la femme du pasteur Wolff ne se soit jamais assise dans le siège en osier, la cuisine est à peu près la même qu'à son époque.*

Pieter de Hooch, Mut-
ter mit Kind, das den
Kopf in ihren Schoß legt
(um 1658–1660): Wird
das Kind sich später je
an seinen ersten Liebes-
kummer erinnern?

Pieter de Hooch, A Mo-
ther and Child, with
its Head in her Lap
(c. 1658–1660): Will this
child look back one day
on her first disappoint-
ment in love?

Pieter de Hooch, Mère
et son enfant, la tête
sur ses genoux (vers
1658–1660): L'enfant
se souviendra-t-elle,
un jour, de son premier
chagrin d'amour?

Ein ganz mit Delfter
Kacheln verkleideter
Kamin und ein Alkoven
mit karmesinrotem Vor-
hang: Wer möchte in
diesem einladenden
Zimmer nicht gerne die
Nacht verbringen?

A warm and welcoming
bedroom, with a fire-
place entirely faced in
Delft tiles and a crim-
son-curtained bed-recess
– what better place to
spend the night?

Une cheminée habillée
de carreaux de Delft et
un lit d'alcôve drapé de
rideaux cramoisis: qui
refuserait de passer la
nuit dans cette chambre
chaude et accueillante?

HET OUDE VEERHUIS

Marieke Brandsma en Rob Bruil

De Betuwe

Das bescheidene reetgedeckte Häuschen, in dem Marieke Brandsma und Rob Bruil und ihre Kinder Joris und Bastiaan ein Zuhause gefunden haben, schmiegt sich an den Deich, der die Felder um Varik vor dem Hochwasser des Flusses Waal schützen soll. Die Lage war ein zusätzlicher Anreiz, sich für die im 18. Jahrhundert erbaute ehemalige Unterkunft des Brückenwächters zu entscheiden. Rob, ein begabter Restaurator und Antiquitätenhändler und seiner Frau gefiel das Haus auf Anhieb so sehr, daß sie es spontan kauften. Dabei spielte der Wunsch, dem Stadtleben den Rücken zu kehren, in der freien Natur zu leben und in einem Haus zu wohnen, das ihre wunderbare Sammlung alter Möbel und Objekte perfekt zur Geltung bringt, eine große Rolle. Im Laufe etlicher Jahre haben die Bruils eine bemerkenswerte Kollektion an Stühlen, Schränken, Utensilien, Gemälden und dekorativen Kunstobjekten zusammengetragen, die ihre Liebe zu den Traditionen und dem holländischen Kunsthandwerk widerspiegelt. Und da es ihnen ein Anliegen ist, die Vergangenheit wieder aufleben zu lassen, wirkt »Het Oude Veerhuis« mit seinem bezaubernden Garten heute genauso schön wie in seiner einstigen Blütezeit.

VORHERGEHENDE DOPPELSEITE: *Das alte Fährhaus vom mit Buchsbaum, Lavendel und Alchemilla vulgaris bepflanzten Garten aus gesehen. Auf dem Deich erkennt man die Silhouette vom »Dikke Toren«, dem mächtigen Turm von Varik.*
LINKS: *Joris und Bastiaan spielen gern am Hang des Deichs.*

PRECEDING PAGES: *"Het Oude Veerhuis", seen from the formal garden (box, lavender and Alchemilla vulgaris). On the dyke, the silhouette of the "Dikke Toren" (the squat tower) of Varik.*
LEFT: *Joris and Bastiaan playing on the grassy slope of the dyke.*

DOUBLE PAGE PRÉCÉDENTE: *«Het Oude Veerhuis» vu du jardin formel planté de buis, de lavande et d'alchémille. Sur la digue, on aperçoit la silhouette du «Dikke Toren», la Grosse Tour, de Varik.*
A GAUCHE: *Joris et Bastiaan adorent jouer dans l'herbe sur le flanc de la digue.*

Marieke Brandsma and Rob Bruil live with their children
Joris and Bastiaan in a modest thatched farmhouse, huddled
against the dyke which protects the fields around Varik from
flooding by the River Waal. It's easy to understand how this
18th-century bridge keeper's lodge cast its spell on the Bruils.
Rob, a gifted restorer and antique dealer, and his wife bought
the house on impulse, but the desire to get out of town and
take refuge in a country place which could contain their magnificent collection of old furniture and objects may also have
had something to do with the decision. Over many years,
the Bruils have accumulated a remarkable stock of chairs,
wardrobes, utensils, paintings and decorative objects that reflects their love of traditional skills and Dutch folklore. And
because they can't resist recreating the past in some measure,
"Het Oude Veerhuis" and its ravishing garden offer a mirror
image of a real period décor.

La modeste fermette au toit de chaume où habitent Marieke
Brandsma et Rob Bruil et leurs enfants Joris et Bastiaan est
blottie contre la digue qui sépare les champs s'étendant autour
de Varik de la rivière Waal toujours menacée de crue. On
comprend aisément pourquoi ils ont été séduits par cet ancien
gîte de pontier construit au 18e siècle. Rob, un antiquaire et
restaurateur de grand talent, et sa femme ont acheté la maison
sur un coup de foudre, mais le désir de fuir la ville, de se réfu-
gier en pleine campagne et de vivre dans une demeure qui
ferait ressortir à merveille leur belle collection de meubles et
d'objets anciens, a joué aussi un rôle très important. Depuis
de longues années, les Bruil ont amassé un ensemble remarquable de sièges, d'armoires, d'ustensiles divers, de tableaux et
d'objets d'art qui reflètent leur goût pour les anciennes traditions et pour un artisanat puisant son inspiration dans le folklore des Pays-Bas. Comme ils ne peuvent s'empêcher de recréer le passé, «Het Oude Veerhuis» et son ravissant jardin
offrent l'image parfaite d'un décor d'époque.

LINKE SEITE: *Vor der Tür, die zu den Schlafzimmern führt, ziehen ein geschnitztes hölzernes Karussellpferd aus dem 18. Jahrhundert und ein Kabinenkoffer aus der gleichen Epoche den Blick auf sich.*
OBEN: *Im Wohnzimmer hat Rob Bruil alte Holzdielen verlegt, die früher zur Lagerung von Käse dienten.*
RECHTS: *Ein »stick chair«, ein rustikaler Stuhl aus Wales, hat seinen idealen Platz neben einer Anrichte aus Huizen gefunden, deren Material wie Holz wirkt.*

FACING PAGE: *near the door leading to the bedrooms, a wooden horse from an 18th-century merry-go-round, and a ship's chest from the same period.*
ABOVE: *In the drawing room, Rob Bruil has laid floorboards made of old planks once used for stacking Dutch cheeses.*
RIGHT: *a Welsh stick chair neatly positioned beside a faux-bois sideboard from Huizen.*

PAGE DE GAUCHE: *Près de la porte qui mène vers les chambres à coucher, un cheval de manège 18e en bois sculpté et une malle de cabine de la même époque attirent le regard.*
CI-DESSUS: *Dans le séjour, Rob Bruil a posé un plancher composé d'anciens rayons en bois qui servaient jadis à entreposer des fromages.*
A DROITE: *Une «stick chair», une chaise rustique provenant du Pays de Galles, a trouvé sa place à côté d'un buffet en faux bois originaire de Huizen.*

OBEN: *Die beiden in einem Holzrahmen gefaßten Moskitonetze aus dem 18. Jahrhundert schützen die Bruils vor den Blicken der vereinzelten Passanten.*
RECHTS: *In der Küche hat der »spinde«, ein bemalter Holzschrank aus dem 19. Jahrhundert aus dem Ort Staphorst (Region Overijssel), einen Ehrenplatz.*
RECHTE SEITE: *Die Küche wirkt authentisch. Den Bruils gefiel es, sie mit alten Küchenutensilien und lackierten Vorratsdosen aus Blech aus dem 19. Jahrhundert zu dekorieren.*

ABOVE: *A pair of 18th-century carved wooden screens protect the Bruils from the prying eyes of passers-by.*
RIGHT: *in the kitchen, a "spinde" – a 19th-century painted wooden cupboard – from the village of Staphorst (province of Overijssel) – takes a place of honour.*
FACING PAGE: *The kitchen is entirely authentic: The Bruils had fun decorating it with old utensils and 19th-century painted food tins.*

CI-DESSUS: *Une paire de moustiquaires 18ᵉ, au cadre en bois sculpté, protègent les Bruil des regards indiscrets des rares passants.*
A DROITE: *Dans la cuisine, une «spinde» – une armoire en bois peint 19ᵉ provenant du village de Staphorst (province d'Overijssel) – occupe une place de choix.*
PAGE DE DROITE: *La cuisine respire l'authenticité et les Bruil se sont amusés à la décorer d'ustensiles anciens et de boîtes à provisions 19ᵉ en tôle peinte.*

ARNO VERHOEVEN EN JAAP ECKHARDT

Friesland

Als sie ihr Haus im Süden Hollands aufgaben und sich für einen großen verfallenen Bauernhof in Friesland entschieden, ließen sich die Antiquitätenhändler Arno Verhoeven und Jaap Eckhardt auf ein waghalsiges Abenteuer ein. Enge Freunde konnten sich nicht erklären, was in aller Welt sie dazu getrieben hatte, sich in einem Kaff mit dem seltsamen, fast unaussprechlichen Namen Pingjum niederzulassen. Heute erklären Arno und Jaap ihre erstaunliche Kehrtwendung mit Liebe auf den ersten Blick für das weite flache Land im Norden. Aber wenn sie auf dieses alte Bauernhaus, das als Café genutzt wurde, zu sprechen kommen und von ihren Mühen mit den Sperrholztrennwänden, den Lampen und der Farbgebung im schlechtesten 1970er-Jahre-Stil erzählen, wirkt der Entschluss, ihr schönes Biedermeier-Haus zugunsten eines architektonischen Horrortrips aufzugeben, wie Masochismus … Ohne Arnos Talent und den körperlichen Einsatz von Jaap, aber vor allem ohne die zahlreichen Funde wie die dekorativen alten Vertäfelungen, der falsche Marmor, die traditionellen Farben, gefliesten Böden, Trompe-l'Œil-Tapeten und die für die Region typischen Matratzenstoffe hätte das Abenteuer fehlschlagen können. Aber dank ihres Weitblicks und ihrer Ausdauer wurde das Dorf Pingjum in einer entlegenen Ecke Frieslands vor dem Vergessen bewahrt.

Das knallrote Innenleben des Schranks passt perfekt zu dem gestreiften Bezug des Empire-Sofas.

The bright red interior of the wardrobe goes perfectly with the striped mattress ticking which covers the Empire sofa.

L'intérieur rouge vif de l'armoire se marie parfaitement avec le tissu à matelas rayé qui recouvre le canapé Empire.

When they exchanged their house in southern Holland for a large dilapidated farm in Friesland, the antique dealers Arno Verhoeven and Jaap Eckhardt launched themselves into a quixotic adventure. Their friends wondered why on earth they had decided to bury themselves in this unpronounceable place called Pingjum. Today Arno and Jaap explain their conduct by describing how smitten they were from the first moment they laid eyes on the wide northern plains. But when they reveal their trials with the former café annexe they now call home, and tell of their battles with plywood partitions and lamps and colours in the worst 1970s taste, their reasons for leaving a beautiful Biedermeier house for an architectural horror seem tantamount to masochism. Had it not been for Arno's talent, Jaap's hard work, and the decorative finds they made between them – such as period panelling, "faux-marbre", traditional colours, flagstones on the floors, trompe- l'œil wallpaper designs and locally-made mattress ticking – the adventure would surely have turned disastrous. As it is, thanks to their perseverance the village of Pingjum in remotest Friesland has been saved from oblivion.

En quittant leur maison située dans le sud de la Hollande pour une grande ferme délabrée en Frise, les antiquaires Arno Verhoeven et Jaap Eckhardt se sont lancés dans une aventure rocambolesque. Leurs amis intimes se sont demandés pourquoi ils avaient décidé d'aller s'enterrer dans ce trou perdu au nom bizarre et pratiquement imprononçable de Pingjum. Aujourd'hui Arno et Jaap s'expliquent sur cette volte-face étonnante en décrivant leur coup de foudre pour les vastes plaines du Nord. Mais quand ils dévoilent leurs tribulations avec cette ancienne ferme-café et qu'ils racontent leur bras de fer avec des cloisons en contre-plaqué et avec des luminaires et des coloris dans le plus mauvais goût «seventies», leur décision de quitter une très belle maison Biedermeier pour une horreur architecturale, rassemble a du masochisme ... Sans le talent d'Arno et sans «l'huile de coude» de Jaap et surtout sans leurs trouvailles décoratives: lambris d'époque, faux-marbres, coloris traditionnels, papiers peints en trompe-l'œil, sols dallés et tissus à matelas typiques de la région, l'aventure aurait pu tourner au désastre. Grâce à leur perspicacité et à leur persévérance, le village de Pingjum, au fin fond de la Frise, a été tiré de l'oubli.

An dem schwarzen Zaun, der den Garten umgibt, macht das Fragment einer alten Gipsmaske neugierig.

On the black fence surrounding the garden, a fragment of a plaster mask creates an intriguing detail.

Sur la clôture noire qui entoure le jardin, un fragment de masque en plâtre ancien attise la curiosité.

OBEN: *Bemalte Empire-Vertäfelungen, zwei holländische Holztüren mit Louis-Seize-Schnitzereien und zahlreiche weiße Delfter Kacheln, so genannte »witjes«, prägen die Einrichtung des Salons.*
RECHTS: *Vor der Wandvertäfelung steht eine Sèvres-Vase aus dem 19. Jahrhundert.*
RECHTE SEITE: *Arno hat den deutschen Schrank aus dem 18. Jahrhundert außen blau und innen in seiner Lieblingsfarbe Geranienrot gestrichen. Die Empire-Möbel stammen aus einem Schloss.*

ABOVE: *The décor of the salon is composed of elements of painted Empire panelling, with two carved Louis-Seize doors (Dutch) and a large number of Delft tiles called "witjes".*
RIGHT: *A 19th-century Sèvres vase is set off by the gray panelling behind.*
FACING PAGE: *Arno covered this 18th-century German wardrobe with a blue wash, and painted the inside in his favourite geranium red. The Empire furniture was salvaged from a castle.*

CI-DESSUS: *Le salon: des éléments de boiserie peintes d'époque Empire, une paire de portes sculptées hollandaises d'époque Louis Seize et de nombreux carreaux en Delft blanc, les «witjes», composent le décor.*
A DROITE: *Un vase en Sèvres 19ᵉ se détache sur un fond de lambris.*
PAGE DE DROITE: *Arno a recouvert l'armoire allemande 18ᵉ d'un lavis bleu et a peint l'intérieur avec son rouge géranium préféré. Le mobilier Empire a été déniché dans un château.*

LINKS: *Es gibt nichts Erfreulicheres für eine verliebte Frau als einen unerwarteten Liebesbrief: Pieter de Hooch, Mann, der einer Frau einen Brief vorliest (um 1670–1674).*

RECHTE SEITE: *Die Küche ist blau-weiß gehalten. Die emaillierten Küchengeräte stammen vom Anfang des 20. Jahrhunderts, die Schränke und der Kaminabzug wurden von Arno gestrichen, die Wände zieren »witjes« und den Boden weiße Fliesen.*

LEFT: *the unexpected arrival of a love letter: Pieter de Hooch, A Man Reading a Letter to a Woman (c. 1670–1674).*

FACING PAGE: *The colours in the kitchen are blue and white, with early 20th-century metal utensils, cupboards and stove hood painted by Arno, walls covered with "witjes", and a white-tiled floor.*

A GAUCHE: *rien de plus doux pour une jeune femme éprise que la visite inattendue d'un messager d'amour: Pieter de Hooch, Homme lisant une lettre à une femme (vers 1670–1674).*

PAGE DE DROITE: *Dans la cuisine, la palette est bleue et blanche: ustensiles de cuisine en métal émaillé début 20e, placards et hotte de cheminée peints par Arno, murs revêtus de «witjes» et carreaux blancs sur le sol.*

$\mathcal{D}$ELAGRADÈRE

Bella en Hans Hesseling

Noord-Holland

Jean Cocteau sagte einmal: »Kreativität entsteht durch Hindernisse« und es hat den Anschein, als sei diese Erkenntnis Grundlage für den Einfallsreichtum des Dekorateurs Hans Hesseling. Hans und seine Frau Bella leben im östlichen Friesland in einem außergewöhnlichen Haus, das von einem sehr schönen Garten und weiten Wiesen umgeben ist. Wenn man durch das riesige Tor am Eingang tritt, gelangt man in ein Reich der optischen Täuschungen. Hesseling gesteht gerne, dass es sich bei seinem Besitz um eine Art dreidimensionales Trompe- l'Œil handelt, das er eigenhändig erschaffen hat. Das gilt für das schöne Haus im reinsten holländischen Stil des 18. Jahrhunderts, die vertäfelten Innenräume, den größten Teil der Möbel und sogar die korallenfarbene Rocaille-Bank aus Beton im Garten mit den Buchsbaumhecken. Steckt Hans Hesselings Ideenreichtum auch hinter dem Schrankbett, das einem der Gemälde von Pieter de Hooch entsprungen sein könnte? Hat er den Kronleuchter – scheinbar aus dem 18. Jahrhundert – tatsächlich aus Karton, Glaskristallen und Plastikröhren angefertigt? Hesseling amüsiert sich über die Verwirrung seiner Besucher und erklärt beharrlich, er habe lediglich auf »einige Holzteile und originelle Ideen« zurückgegriffen. Genauso ungewöhnlich ist seine Devise »Ubi bene, ibi patria« – nach Cicero: »Da wo ich mich wohl fühle, ist meine Heimat«.

Bei Hesseling ist alles Illusion: Die orangerote Gartenbank mit den geschwungenen Formen besteht aus Beton.

For Hesseling, illusion is the norm – even his red-orange baroque garden bench is made of concrete.

Pour Hesseling, tout est illusion, et le banc de jardin aux formes baroques, couleur rouge orange, est en béton.

Wer hätte vermutet, dass es »Delagradère« erst seit knapp 25 Jahren gibt?

Who would imagine that "Delagradère" is barely 25 years old?

Qui pourrait soupçonner que «Delagradère» a à peine plus d'un quart de siècle?

Jean Cocteau used to say that difficulty stimulates creativity and we wonder if this maxim applies especially to the decorator Hans Hesseling. Hans and his wife Bella live in a remarkable house surrounded by a beautiful garden and the broad fields of eastern Friesland. When you pass through the monumental gate you enter a domain which is dedicated to the art of optical illusion, and Hesseling himself admits that his house is no more than a three-dimensional *trompe-l'œil*, one that he has constructed entirely with his own hands. This is quite an achievement, given that the building seems to be pure 18th-century Dutch. Yet everything here, including the panelling, most of the furniture and objects, and the "rocaille" bench, coral-hued but made of concrete, which overlooks the box *parterre*, is authentically fake. Hans is also the creator of the box-bed, which seems straight out of a painting by Pieter de Hooch. But did he really make the 18th-century chandelier out of cardboard, glass pendants and bits of plastic pipe? Ask him and he grins. Yes, he began with a few pieces of wood and some original ideas – as original in their way as the name of the house, Delagradère, and his motto "Ubi bene, ibi patria": "Wherever I am happy, there my country is."

In seinem Alkoven mit sonnenblumengelben Damastvorhängen posiert Hans Hesseling nach Art der Alten Meister.

In his bed with its sunflower-yellow damask hangings, Hans Hesseling does his best to look like a character out of an old painting.

Dans son lit-alcôve aux rideaux en soie damassée jaune tournesol, Hans Hesseling fait de son mieux pour ressembler à un personnage de tableau ancien.

Jean Cocteau disait: «C'est l'empêchement qui fait créer», et on se demande si cette idée sous-tend la démarche du décorateur Hans Hesseling. Hans et son épouse Bella habitent une maison exceptionnelle entourée d'un très beau jardin et de vastes prairies dans la Frise de l'est. En poussant la grille monumentale, on a l'impression d'entrer dans un domaine voué à l'art de la tricherie visuelle. Hesseling est le premier à avouer que sa demeure n'est rien d'autre qu'un trompe-l'œil en trois dimensions et qu'il a tout réalisé de ses propres mains: la jolie maison dans le plus pur style 18ᵉ hollandais, les intérieurs tapissés de lambris, la plus grande partie des meubles et des objets et même le banc «rocaille» couleur corail en béton qui domine le parterre en buis taillé devant la maison. Comment? Est-il aussi responsable du lit armoire qui aurait pu figurer sur un tableau de Pieter de Hooch? A-t-il vraiment fabriqué le lustre «18ᵉ» avec du carton, des pampilles de verre et des fragments de tuyau en plastique? Hesseling se délecte de l'incrédulité de ses visiteurs et répète qu'il n'a eu recours qu'à «quelques bouts de bois et des idées originales». Aussi originales d'ailleurs que sa devise «Ubi bene, ibi patria» empruntée à Cicéron – «Où l'on est bien, là est la patrie».

OBEN: *Der große Salon steht im Zeichen der perfekten Symmetrie: Vertäfelungen im Stil des 18. Jahrhunderts, perfekt eingepasste Vitrinen und zeitgenössische Pastelltöne.*
RECHTS: *Den schönen Louis-Seize-Eckschrank hat Hans außen in Pastelltönen und innen knallrot gestrichen.*
RECHTE SEITE: *Im Vorzimmer ist alles neu: die Vertäfelungen in rosa und blassrot, die aufgemalte Verzierung über dem Kamin, der Ofen, der Stuhl und sogar die Delfter Vasen auf dem Kaminsims!*

ABOVE: *Perfect symmetry predominates in the main living room: 18th-century style panels, glass-fronted cupboards, and period pastel colours.*
RIGHT: *a fine Louis-Seize corner cupboard, painted on the outside in pastel tones and on the inside a bright red.*
FACING PAGE: *In the antechamber, everything is brand new: the faded pink and red panels, the painted decoration on the fireplace, the stove, the chair and even the pair of Delfi vases on the chimney-piece.*

CI-DESSUS: *Dans le grand salon règne une symétrie parfaite – lambris façon 18ᵉ, vitrines et portes au sommet chantourné et couleurs pastel d'époque.*
A DROITE: *Hans a peint une belle encoignure d'époque Louis Seize dans des tons pastel et badigeonné l'intérieur de rouge vif.*
PAGE DE DROITE: *Dans l'antichambre tout est neuf: les lambris rose et rouge fané, la décoration peinte de la cheminée, le poêle, la chaise et même la paire de potiches en Delft sur la tablette de l'âtre!*

HET OUDE WEESHUIS

Yvonne en Edgar Bijvoet van den Abbeelen

Noord-Holland

Zweifellos glich das alte Waisenhaus, in dem die Antiquitätenhändlerin Yvonne Bijvoet van den Abbeelen und ihr Mann Edgar heute wohnen, schon im 17. Jahrhundert einem Gemälde von Pieter de Hooch. Und auch heute hat der hübsche Bau aus dem Jahr 1633, der aus mehreren Gebäuden um einen schlichten Innenhof besteht, nichts von seinem pittoresken Charakter eingebüßt. Yvonne, eine spontane, fröhliche junge Frau, hatte sich auf die Suche nach einem Haus gemacht, das sich als Verkaufsraum und Wohnstätte für ihre Familie eignen sollte. Als sie dieses Labyrinth aus heruntergekommenen Zimmern begutachtete, war es Liebe auf den ersten Blick. Mit Hilfe ihres Mannes, ihres Sohnes und des Schreiners Hotze Mul stürzte sie sich in das Unterfangen, das verfallene Waisenhaus zu renovieren und die chaotischen Einzelräume in ein Haus voller Charme zu verwandeln. Da sie das Herz auf der Zunge trägt, berichtet sie freimütig von ihren zahlreichen »Bastelarbeiten« und ihren verrückten Touren durchs ganze Land auf der Suche nach Balken, Bodenbelägen, alten Türen und möglichst authentischen Möbeln. Auf das Ergebnis kann sie zu Recht stolz sein. Sie ist jetzt glücklich in diesem einladenden Haus zu wohnen, das sie mit eigenen Händen wiederhergestellt und mit ihren Fundstücken bereichert hat.

Es ist Herbst und welkes Laub weht durch die Tür, die in den Hof führt.

Autumn leaves by the French windows overlooking the courtyard.

C'est l'automne et les feuilles mortes entrent par la porte-fenêtre donnant sur la cour.

Even in the 17th century, this charming red brick orphanage must already have resembled a painting by Pieter de Hooch. Constructed in 1633, it consists of several buildings around a modest inner courtyard and is occupied today by the antique dealer Yvonne Bijvoet van den Abbeelen and her husband Edgar. Yvonne, a cheerful, spontaneous young woman, was actively searching for a large townhouse where she could have a shop and raise a family. But when she saw the orphanage's labyrinth of crumbling rooms she was completely smitten. Helped by her husband and son and seconded by a gifted carpenter, Hotze Mul, she grappled with the ruined orphanage and succeeded in transforming its original chaos into a house of great charm. Yvonne wears her heart on her sleeve; she admits to combing the Netherlands in search of the beams, floorboards, old doors and furniture, which would eventually lend total authenticity to her décor. And she has a right to be proud of the result, and to feel happy in this warm and welcoming place, rebuilt with her own hands and filled with her own discoveries.

Die verspielte Yvonne liebt Hirschgeweihe.

Yvonne, mischievous as ever, has a special fondness for stags' horns.

Yvonne adore les bois de cerf et elle les manipule avec son espièglerie habituelle.

Au 17ᵉ siècle, le vieil orphelinat qu'occupent aujourd'hui l'antiquaire Yvonne Bijvoet van den Abbeelen et son mari Edgar, ressemblait sans aucun doute à un tableau de Pieter de Hooch. De nos jours, cette charmante bâtisse en briques rouges, érigée en 1633, et qui est composée de plusieurs bâtiments autour d'une modeste cour intérieure, n'a rien perdu de son caractère pittoresque. Yvonne, une jeune femme rieuse et spontanée, était partie à l'époque à la recherche d'une grande maison bourgeoise où elle pourrait à la fois tenir boutique et installer sa famille, mais c'est en visitant ce labyrinthe de pièces vétustes, qu'elle fut prise d'un coup de foudre. Assistée par son mari et par son fils et secondée par celui qu'elle appelle «un menuisier de grand talent», le fidèle Hotze Mul, elle s'attaqua à son orphelinat en ruine et réussit à transformer cet ensemble chaotique en une maison pleine de charme. Comme elle a le cœur sur la langue, elle avoue volontiers ses multiples «bricolages» et ses folles randonnées à travers le pays pour trouver les poutres, les planchers, les vieilles portes et le mobilier qui allaient contribuer à l'authenticité du décor. Elle a tout à fait raison d'être fière du résultat et de se sentir heureuse dans cette demeure hospitalière qu'elle a reconstruite de ses propres mains et où s'amoncellent ses trouvailles.

Im Innenhof verschwinden die alten Mauern hinter einer üppigen Glyzinie.

In the courtyard, the old walls are almost entirely obscured by wistaria.

Dans la cour, les vieux murs disparaissent sous une glycine envahissante.

OBEN: *Jan Vermeer, Herr und Dame beim Wein (um 1658–1660): Er suchte sie auf, um sie mit Musik zu erfreuen und sie einen prickelnden Rheinwein kosten zu lassen.*

ABOVE: *Jan Vermeer, The Glass of Wine (c. 1658–1660): The visitor brings music – and a glass of delicious sparkling wine.*

CI-DESSUS: *Jan Vermeer, Le verre de vin (vers 1658–1660): Il est venu pour lui jouer de la musique et lui faire goûter un vin du Rhin pétillant.*

FACING PAGE: *A light reminiscent of Vermeer floods across the 19th-century armchair with its antique fabric. The "painting" on the wall is in reality a fragment of Cordoba leather stuck in a frame.*

RECHTE SEITE: *Das berühmte Vermeer-Licht umspielt einen Sessel aus dem 19. Jahrhundert mit altem Bezug. Das »Gemälde« an der Wand entpuppt sich als ein Stück gerahmtes Cordoba-Leder.*

PAGE DE DROITE: *Une lumière à la Vermeer inonde un fauteuil 19ᵉ revêtu d'un tissu ancien. Le «tableau» au mur n'est autre qu'un fragment de cuir de Cordoue encadré.*

BERGERAC
Jan des Bouvrie
Noord-Holland

Als er noch kurze Hosen trug, fuhr der heutige Guru des holländischen Designs, Jan des Bouvrie, oft mit dem Fahrrad zu der herrlichen Villa, die der Architekt Boissevain im Jahr 1911 gebaut hatte, und schwor sich, dass die »Villa Bergerac« eines Tages ihm gehören sollte. Seine Eltern waren große Liebhaber des Designs des 20. Jahrhunderts und verkauften in ihrem kleinen Geschäft in Bussum im Süden von Amsterdam Avantgarde-Möbel, Lampen und Objekte. Jan wurde zu einem der wichtigsten Designer der Nachkriegszeit und abgesehen von seiner ungewöhnlichen Erscheinung – lockiges Haar, lachende Augen und Fliege – kennen und lieben die Holländer ihn, weil er das berühmte »Kubus«-Sofa entworfen hat und mit seiner modernen Formensprache der Inneneinrichtung neuen Schwung gab. Jans Kindheitstraum wurde übrigens schon vor langer Zeit Wirklichkeit und in seiner Villa, die er wie einen Schatz hütet, konnte er seine kühnsten Dekorationsideen umsetzen. Unterstützt von seiner Frau Monique verfeinert des Bouvrie unablässig den klassischen Bau und den dazugehörigen weitläufigen englischen Park. In dem Spannungsfeld zwischen Gestern und Heute finden Barockkonsolen, ein Rokokospiegel und ein gustavianischer Lüster ebenso Platz wie Werke von Picasso und Warhol oder Sessel des ausgehenden 20. Jahrhunderts.

LINKS: *Die Vorhanghalter in Löwenkopfform hat der Hausherr, der im Zeichen des Königs der Tiere geboren ist, selbst entworfen.*
OBEN: *Ein Löwe aus Bronze bewacht die Freitreppe.*

LEFT: *The curtain loops in the shape of lions' heads were made by Jan des Bouvrie, born under the sign of Leo.*
ABOVE: *A bronze lion stands guard on the terrace.*

A GAUCHE: *Les embrasses en forme de tête de lion sont une création du maître de maison, né sous le signe du roi des animaux.*
CI-DESSUS: *Un lion en bronze monte la garde sur le perron.*

As a boy, Jan des Bouvrie, who is now the guru of Dutch design, often bicycled over from his home to gaze at a certain magnificent house. At the time he swore to himself that one day he would own the "Villa Bergerac", built in 1911 by the architect Boissevain. Des Bouvrie's own parents were fascinated by 20th-century design and traded in "avantgarde" furniture, lamps and accessories in their modest shop at Bussum, south of Amsterdam, so it's little wonder that their son later became one of the most important post-war influences in the field. Apart from his physical presence – curly hair, laughing eyes and bow tie – the Dutch know and acknowledge him as the creator of the famous "Kubus" sofa, and for having given new shapes to their interiors. Jan's childhood dream came true some time ago, and he has used his treasured Villa to try out some of his more daring decorative ideas. Helped by his wife Monique, des Bouvrie is constantly refining the classical architecture of the house. He is fascinated by juxtapositions of past and present, with the result that at Bergerac you will find works by Andy Warhol paired with baroque consoles, Picasso jostling with a rocaille mirror, and an authentic Gustavian chandelier hovering over clusters of chairs made in the year 2000.

Bereits am Eingang kündigen die Formen eine Kombination aus der nüchternen Architektur der 1930er Jahre und gotischen Elementen an.

In the front doorway are shapes that already suggest the pared-down architecture of the 1930s, along with more Gothic elements.

Dans l'entrée, des formes qui annoncent déjà l'architecture dépouillée des années 1930 se marient avec des éléments gothiques.

Quand il portait encore des culottes courtes, le «gourou» du design hollandais, Jan des Bouvrie, faisait souvent un tour à bicyclette pour aller s'asseoir dans l'herbe face à une splendide résidence, et il se jurait qu'un jour la «Villa Bergerac» lui appartiendrait. Ses parents étaient passionnés par le design du 20ᵉ siècle et vendaient des meubles, des lampes et des accessoires d'avant-garde dans leur modeste magasin à Bussum, au sud d'Amsterdam. Jan devint l'un des designers les plus importants de l'après-guerre et, mis à part sa présence physique – cheveux bouclés, yeux rieurs et nœud papillon –, les Hollandais le connaissent – et lui en sont reconnaissants – pour avoir créé le célèbre canapé «Kubus» et avoir donné une forme nouvelle à tout ce qui touche à leur maison, leur intérieur et leur confort. Le rêve d'enfant de Jan s'est réalisé depuis longtemps et, dans ce Bergerac qu'il couve comme un trésor rare, il a pu réaliser ses idées décoratives les plus audacieuses. Secondé par sa femme Monique, des Bouvrie n'arrête pas de peaufiner cette architecture classique, construite en 1911 par Boissevain, et le vaste parc à l'anglaise qui l'entoure. Comme il jure par le contraste fascinant entre «hier» et «aujourd'hui», les consoles baroques se marient avec Warhol, Picasso avec un miroir rocaille et un lustre gustavien avec des sièges de la fin du 20ᵉ siècle.

Ein steinerner Apollo versteckt sich hinter einem Torbogen aus Buchsbaum.

A stone Apollo hides behind a box-hedge archway.

Un Apollon en pierre se cache derrière une haie en buis taillé auquel on a donné la forme d'une arche carrée.

OBEN: *Jan des Bouvrie kombinierte ohne zu zögern zwei vergoldete barocke Konsolen mit »Starporträts« von Christopher Makos und dem Spiralsofa von Edra.*

RECHTS: *Ein später Sonnenstrahl verweilt auf einem orangefarben bezogenen Sessel. Das Gemälde stammt von Berend Hoekstra.*

RECHTE SEITE: *Der Sohn Jantje widmet sich Schokoladenkeksen. Sein Kinderstuhl ist eine humorvolle Parodie auf den holländischen Stil.*

ABOVE: *Without a qualm, Jan des Bouvrie has juxtaposed a pair of baroque gilded pier-tables with portraits of "stars" by Christopher Makos and a spiral sofa by Edra.*

RIGHT: *A late ray of sunshine lingers on an armchair covered with an orange fabric. The painting is by Berend Hoekstra.*

FACING PAGE: *Jantje, Jan des Bouvrie's son, attends to the chocolate biscuits. The high chair is a comical parody of the traditional Dutch style.*

CI-DESSUS: *Des Bouvrie n'hésite pas à marier une paire de consoles dorées baroques avec des portraits de «stars» signés Christopher Makos et à donner une place de choix au canapé-spirale d'Edra.*

A DROITE: *Un rayon de soleil tardif s'attarde sur un fauteuil recouvert d'un tissu orange. Le tableau est signé Berend Hoekstra.*

PAGE DE DROITE: *Le fils des Bouvrie — Jantje — se gave de biscuits au chocolat. Sa chaise haute est une parodie pleine d'humour sur le style hollandais.*

HILLENIUSSINGEL

Han Adriaanse

Zuid-Holland

Vor gut zehn Jahren kaufte der Innenarchitekt Han Adriaanse die Hälfte einer alten Dorfschule in der Nähe von Rotterdam, die Anfang des 20. Jahrhunderts erbaut worden war – ein nicht gerade alltägliches Objekt mit vielen großen Räumen. Wo sich einst die Schüler mit dem Alphabet und dem Einmaleins herumgeschlagen haben, stieß der Architekt nun auf ganz andere Probleme: ungefähr fünfzig morsche Balken, den völlig ruinierten Boden und eine eindrucksvolle Anzahl von Trennwänden und Zwischendecken, die entfernt werden mussten. Doch Han, ein ehemaliger Restaurator von historischen Gebäuden, verwirklichte sein Vorhaben und verwandelte die Schule schließlich in ein ungewöhnliches Haus. Seinen persönlichen Stil zu beschreiben, ist nicht leicht: Er ist ein Innenarchitekt mit unkonventionellen Ideen und liebt eine Bohème-Atmosphäre, die von dem Charme der Fundstücke und alten Patina lebt. Han macht keinen Hehl daraus, dass er Dinge gerne recycelt, und so hat er für Vertäfelungen und Trennwände sogar Türen aus öffentlichen Toiletten zweckentfremdet. Bei ihm dürfen ein alter Stuhl, die Fragmente einer Hermes-Büste aus Gips und verrostetes Spielzeug ihren Lebensabend verbringen. »Ich mag die Schönheit der Vergänglichkeit«, erklärt er. »Übrigens kann man auch mit alten Dingen eine moderne Atmosphäre schaffen!«

LINKS: *Eine Madonna aus Gips scheint in den Anblick der zahlreichen Objekte in einer Ecke des Ateliers versunken.*
OBEN: *Das Still-Leben wurde aus einem Moskitonetz, einem Kleiderbügel und einem kleinen Buch komponiert.*

LEFT: *A plaster Madonna contemplates the jumble of objects piled in one corner of the studio.*
ABOVE: *still life: a mosquito screen, a coat-hanger, and a book.*

A GAUCHE: *Une vierge en plâtre promène son regard songeur sur les objets hétéroclites entassés dans un coin de l'atelier.*
CI-DESSUS: *nature morte composée d'une moustiquaire, d'un cintre et d'un livre.*

When, ten years ago, the interior architect Han Adriaanse bought half of an early 20th-century school in a village near Rotterdam, he knew he was acquiring a most unusual building of most unusual proportions. Where once the local children had cudgelled their brains over multiplication and the ABC, Adriaanse grappled with rotted beams, imploded floorboards, and partitions and false ceilings that wanted blasting. He imposed his will; and before long he had transformed the old school into a remarkable place to live. The personal style of this former restorer of historic buildings is not easily describable. Suffice it to say that he is a thoroughly unconventional interior architect, who swears by what he calls a "high Bohemian" ambience, in which old patinas and "objets trouvés" tend to predominate. Han has a special fondness for recycling things. He will happily manufacture panels and partitions from the doors of public lavatories; in his hands, a broken chair, odd bits of a plaster bust of Hermes, or an old rusty toy may expect spectacular reprieve. "The beauty I like best is the beauty of decline," says he. "What's more, I maintain that you can create a totally contemporary ambiance with things that are old as the hills."

Im Haus von Han hat das Arrangement der Objekte immer etwas Magisches.

In Han's house, any assemblage of objects tends to have a subtly magical quality.

Dans la maison de Han, l'amoncellement d'objets a toujours quelque chose de magique.

Bei dem Hutständer im Eingangsbereich handelt es sich um einen gusseisernen Baluster eines Treppengeländers aus dem 19. Jahrhundert.

The hat stand in the hall is actually the lower end of a 19th-century cast iron spiral staircase.

Dans l'entrée, le porte-chapeau n'est autre qu'un départ d'escalier en fonte, datant du 19ᵉ siècle.

En achetant, il y a bien dix ans de cela, la moitié d'une vieille école construite au début du 20ᵉ siècle dans un village près de Rotterdam, l'architecte d'intérieur Han Adriaanse a mis la main sur un bâtiment hors du commun et un ensemble de locaux aux proportions généreuses. A l'endroit même où des élèves appliqués ânonnaient l'alphabet et les tables de multiplication, l'architecte s'est débattu avec une multitude de problèmes, une cinquantaine de poutres complètement pourries, des planchers en état de ruine et un nombre impressionnant de cloisons et de faux plafonds à démolir. Finalement, il a réussi à imposer sa volonté et à transformer l'école en une maison exceptionnelle. Décrire le style de cet ancien restaurateur de bâtiments historiques n'est pas facile. Voilà un architecte d'intérieur aux idées peu conventionnelles et qui ne jure que par une ambiance «haute-bohème» où dominent les patines anciennes et les charmes de l'objet trouvé. Han ne se cache pas d'adorer le recyclage, il n'a pas hésité à fabriquer des lambris et des cloisons avec les portes des toilettes publiques et, chez lui, une chaise caduque, des fragments d'un buste d'Hermès en plâtre et des vieux jouets rouillés ont droit à une seconde vie ... «J'adore la beauté du déclin», dit-il. «D'ailleurs, j'insiste sur le fait qu'on peut créer une ambiance contemporaine avec des matériaux anciens.»

OBEN: *Die Dimensionen des Ateliers lassen auf seine Vergangenheit schließen. Der Boden ist rötlich lackiert, der Tisch in der Ecke des »Esszimmers« besteht aus einer schmiedeeisernen Gartenurne und einer schweren Steinplatte.*

RECHTS: *Hier werden sogar die kleinen Missgeschicke zu Kunstwerken. Aus den Fragmenten einer Hermes-Büste entstand ein Still-Leben.*

RECHTE SEITE: *Die Farbgebung des Bodens in der Eingangshalle erinnert an Marmorplatten.*

ABOVE: *The proportions of the studio betray its past, the floorboards are covered in a reddish varnish and the table in the dining area consists of a cast-iron garden urn with a heavy stone slab on top.*

RIGHT: *another accidental work of art: fragments of a bust of Hermes.*

FACING PAGE: *The boards in the hallway have been painted like a black and white marble floor.*

CI-DESSUS: *Les proportions de l'atelier trahissent sa destination première, le plancher a été recouvert d'un vernis rougeâtre et la table du coin «salle à manger» est une urne de jardin en fonte coiffée d'un lourd plateau de pierre.*

A DROITE: *Même les petits accidents se transforment en œuvres d'art. En témoignent les fragments d'un buste d'Hermès, devenu nature morte par la force des choses.*

PAGE DE DROITE: *Le plancher du hall d'entrée a été peint à la façon d'un dallage de marbre.*

Die Wände des kleinen
Salons sind mit Land-
karten bedeckt und bei
dem »gekachelten« Bo-
den handelt es sich um
eine Trompe-l'Œil-Ma-
lerei. Der Erfindungs-
reichtum von Han
Adriaanse kennt keine
Grenzen …

The walls of the small
salon are covered with
maps and the cabochons
on the floor are trompe-
l'œil painted directly
onto the floorboards.

Les murs d'un petit
salon sont couverts de
mappemondes et le sol
à cabochons n'est autre
qu'un plancher peint en
trompe-l'œil. L'esprit
inventif de Han
Adriaanse ne connaît
pas de limites …

$\mathcal{S}$ LOT ZUYLEN
Belle van Zuylen

Utrecht

»Es gefällt mir gut, keiner Fahne zu folgen, sondern in aller Freiheit durch das Land der Literatur zu spazieren. Daher sind mir Straßenräuber auch lieber als Soldaten«, schrieb Isabelle van Tuyll van Serooskerken 1800 an ihren Freund Monsieur d'Oleyres. Diese Worte verdeutlichen den rebellischen Charakter der Frau, die als »Belle van Zuylen« in die Geschichte eingehen sollte. 1740 im Schloss von Zuylen bei Utrecht geboren, zeigte sie sich schon sehr jung gleichgültig gegenüber ihrer noblen Herkunft und diktatorischen Anstandsregeln. Sie schockierte ihre Zeitgenossen, als sie eine Karriere als Schriftstellerin anstrebte. Später wurde die intelligente junge Frau, die das Herz von James Boswell gewann und die Neugier von Voltaire weckte, von Maurice-Quentin de la Tour und von Jean-Antoine Houdon in Kunstwerken verewigt. Sie heiratete schließlich Monsieur de Charrière. Doch weder der Umzug in die Schweiz, die Heimat ihres Mannes, noch ihre verhängnisvolle Leidenschaft für Benjamin Constant und ihre letzten traurigen Jahre in Colombier, wo sie 1806 starb, ließen sie die Jugendjahre in Holland und das Schloss ihrer Eltern vergessen. In diesem Schloss, in dem sie so glücklich war, bewahrt man heute sorgfältig ihr Andenken: Jedes Möbelstück und jeder Gegenstand zeugen von ihrer strahlenden Gegenwart.

Ein typisches Bild für die sprichwörtliche Sauberkeit der Holländer: eine Nische mit einem Wasserhahn und einem Wassereimer.

A classic image of proverbial Dutch cleanliness: a niche equipped with a tap and a water bucket.

Caractéristique de la propreté proverbiale des Hollandais: une niche équipée d'un robinet en cuivre et un seau.

In 1800 Isabelle van Tuyll van Serooskerken wrote to her friend Monsieur d'Oleyres: "It pleases me to march under no particular banner. I go where I will in the Land of Letters; and because of this I prefer a brigand to a regular soldier, any day of the year." The words encapsulate the rebellious nature of the woman known to history as "Belle van Zuylen", who was born at Zuylen Castle near Utrecht in 1740. At an early age, Belle showed her complete indifference to convention and her noble descent, scandalising her entourage and contemporaries by embarking on a career as a writer. Later this effervescent girl – who excited the curiosity of Voltaire and the passion of James Boswell, and whose clever face was immortalised by the artists Maurice-Quentin de la Tour and Jean-Antoine Houdon – was married to Monsieur de la Charrière; but neither her departure to Switzerland, nor her destructive passion for Benjamin Constant, nor even the sadness of her last years at Colombier, where she died in 1806, could make her forget her youth in Holland or the castle of her parents. Today the rooms in the house where she was so happy are carefully preserved, to the point where every piece of furniture and every object bears the stamp of her radiant presence.

Der Herbst naht und der wilde Wein, der an den Schlossmauern rankt, verwandelt sich in ein Meer rot gefärbter Blätter.

Autumn colours: a Virginia creeper blankets the walls of the castle.

L'automne est tout proche, et la vigne vierge qui couvre les murs du château se transforme en une avalanche de feuilles écarlates.

Die alte Wasserpumpe in der Speisekammer trägt die Aufschrift »kein Trinkwasser«.

A sign by the pantry pump reads "Water unfit to drink".

Dans l'office, l'ancienne pompe à eau porte l'inscription «eau non potable».

«Cela me plaît bien de ne suivre aucun drapeau et de marcher en toute liberté dans le Pays des Lettres. A cet égard, je préfère les brigands à la force militaire régulière», écrivait Isabelle van Tuyll van Serooskerken en 1800 à son ami Monsieur d'Oleyres. Ces quelques mots témoignent parfaitement du caractère rebelle de celle qui devait entrer dans l'histoire comme la «Belle de Zuylen» et qui naquit en 1740 au Château de Zuylen près d'Utrecht. Toute jeune déjà, Belle se montra indifférente à sa noble ascendance et aux contraintes impératives du «comme il faut». Elle scandalisa son entourage et ses contemporains en choisissant une carrière d'écrivain. Plus tard, cette jeune femme pétillante qui éveilla la curiosité de Voltaire et l'amour de James Boswell, et dont le visage rayonnant d'intelligence fut immortalisé par Maurice-Quentin de la Tour et par Jean-Antoine Houdon épousa Monsieur de Charrière. Cependant, ni son départ pour la Suisse, le pays natal de son époux, ni sa passion funeste pour Benjamin Constant et la tristesse de ses dernières années à Colombier où elle mourut en 1806 ne purent lui faire oublier sa jeunesse en Hollande et le château de ses parents. Ce même château où on conserve aujourd'hui, pieusement, ces quelques pièces où elle fut si heureuse et où chaque meuble et chaque objet témoignent de sa radieuse présence.

LINKS: *Die Tapete im Schlafzimmer von Belle ist authentisch, aber in dem Himmelbett hat die »Rebellin« keine schlaflosen Nächte verbracht.*
RECHTE SEITE: *Auf dem Sekretär aus dem 18. Jahrhundert befinden sich neben Belles Briefen und Manuskripten ein Fächer und ein Medaillon, das einen Scherenschnitt ihres Profils zeigt.*

LEFT: *In Belle's former bedroom, the wallpaper is authentic but the draped daybed is a later addition.*
FACING PAGE: *on the 18th-century desk, letters and manuscripts written by Belle, with a fan and a medallion bearing her profile.*

A GAUCHE: *Dans la chambre à coucher de Belle, le papier peint est authentique mais le lit de repos couronné d'un baldaquin n'a jamais connu les nuits blanches de la «rebelle».*
PAGE DE DROITE: *Sur le secrétaire 18ᵉ reposent des lettres et des manuscrits de la pétillante «Zélide», ainsi qu'un éventail et un médaillon représentant son profil en silhouette.*

RECHTS: *Aus ihrem Arbeitszimmer hatte Belle eine herrliche Aussicht auf den Wassergraben des Schlosses und die Landschaft. Der japanische Paravent stammt aus dem 18. Jahrhundert und trennt die Arbeitsecke vom Waschtisch.*

RIGHT: *From her study, Belle could look out, across the moat to the countryside beyond. The Japanese screen, which divides the work area from the washstand, dates from the 18th-century.*

A DROITE: *De sa chambre de travail, Belle avait une vue imprenable sur les douves du château et sur le paysage. Le paravent japonais date du 18ᵉ siècle et sépare le coin-travail du coin-toilette.*

In der komplett mit »witjes« gekachelten Küche scheint die Zeit stehen geblieben zu sein. Mit etwas Fantasie kann man sich den Duft von Brot vorstellen, das gerade frisch aus dem Ofen kommt, oder das Schwatzen der Angestellten hören, die ein opulentes Mahl vorbereiten.

Time stands still in the kitchen, which is tiled throughout with "witjes". It's easy to imagine this room filled with cooks and servants and the scent of baking bread.

Dans la cuisine entièrement carrelée de «witjes», le temps semble s'être arrêté. Avec un peu d'imagination, on sent l'odeur du pain sortant du four et on entend la conversation animée d'une armée de servantes qui s'affairent à préparer un repas succulent.

LINKE SEITE: *Auf der Arbeitsfläche aus Granit neben dem Steinofen liegen frische Brötchen, Eier und ein Zuckerhut.*

FACING PAGE: *Lying on the granite worktop beside the stone oven are fresh rolls, eggs and a cone of sugar.*

PAGE DE GAUCHE: *Près du four à pain sur le plan de travail en granit, quelqu'un a posé des petits pains frais, des œufs et un cône en sucre.*

OBEN: *Die Besucher erwartet ein gar köstliches Mahl: Floris van Dijck, Gedeckter Tisch/Stilleben mit Käse und Früchten (um 1615).*

ABOVE: *A delicious meal awaits the dinner-guests: Floris van Dijck, Laid Table with Cheese and Fruit (c. 1615).*

CI-DESSUS: *Un repas succulent attend les invités: Floris van Dijck, Table avec fromage et fruits (vers 1615).*

JOOP VAN DEN BRINK

Utrecht

Ende des 19. Jahrhunderts wohnte in dem Haus des Bibliothekars Joop van den Brink die vielköpfige Familie eines Tabakbauers. Doch Tabak wird in der friedlichen Region Amerongen in der Provinz Utrecht schon lange nicht mehr angebaut und Joop teilt sein Heim nur noch mit seinem Papagei Gerrit, einem ungefähr sechzigjährigen schwatzhaften Feinschmecker. Abgesehen von einem Taubenpaar gibt es keine weiteren Vögel im Haus, obwohl die zahlreichen leeren alten Käfige im Eingangsbereich, im Sommersalon, im Gewächshaus und in der Küche den Eindruck vermitteln, der Hausherr fühle sich zu »gefiederten Freunden« besonders hingezogen. Neben Käfigen jeglicher Größe sammelt Joop alles, was an die gute alte Zeit unserer Urgroßeltern erinnert und seine weiß gekachelte Küche ist prall gefüllt mit antiken Möbeln und Küchengeräten. Hier vermutet man das Reich einer weißhaarigen Großmutter mit karierter Schürze, die leckere Zimtkekse backt! Sogar die Farben, die verwaschenen Blautöne, das Ochsenblutrot und Lindgrün, erzählen von der Vergangenheit. Und neben den buchsbaumgesäumten Beeten im Garten hält die silberne »Hexenkugel« aus Glas alles fern, was das Glück und den Frieden im Haus beeinträchtigen könnte ...

LINKS: *Im Gewächshaus gibt es zahlreiche Topfpflanzen und eine Sammlung antiker Vogelkäfige.*
OBEN: *Ein alter Käfig über dem Arbeitstisch beherbergt ein Taubenpärchen.*

LEFT: *The greenhouse contains a multitude of potted plants along with a collection of antique birdcages.*
ABOVE: *a pair of doves in a cage above a work-table.*

A GAUCHE: *La serre abrite un grand nombre de plantes en pot et une collection de cages à oiseaux anciennes.*
CI-DESSUS: *Au-dessus de la table de travail, une vieille cage accueille une paire de colombes.*

Towards the close of the 19th century, the house of the librarian Joop van den Brink was home to a tobacco farmer's extensive family. Since then, the region of Amerongen – a peaceful village which is among the pearls of the province of Utrecht – has seen the gradual eclipse of tobacco as a crop, and as a result Joop shares his house with no-one but a greedy, garrulous sexagenarian parrot named Gerrit. Apart from a pair of doves, there are no other birds in the building; but in the hall, the "salon d'été", the orangery and the kitchen a host of empty cages betray Mr. van den Brink's special love for his winged friends. Apart from cages of every shape and size, Joop collects anything and everything that dates from the time of our great-grandparents. His white-tiled kitchen, jammed with old furniture and utensils, looks like the lair of some adorable grandmother with snow-white hair and checked apron, who spends her every waking hour making delicious cinnamon cakes. Even the colours of the house (washed blue, "sang de boeuf", lime green) speak softly of the past, while in the garden with its borders and box hedges there is a glass "witch's ball" silvered with mercury, whose function is to ward off anything which might threaten the peace of Joop van den Brink.

In dem geometrisch angelegten Gärtchen mit den beschnittenen Buchsbaumumfassungen krönt eine »Hexenkugel« ein schmiedeeisernes Gerüst.

In the formal box garden, a "witch's ball" on a wrought iron mounting.

Dans le jardinet formel avec ses parterres en buis taillé, une armature en fer forgé est couronnée d'une «boule de sorcière».

Vers la fin du 19ᵉ siècle, la maison du bibliothécaire Joop van den Brink abritait la famille nombreuse d'un cultivateur de tabac. Depuis, la région d'Amerongen – un de ces villages si paisibles qui font la richesse de la province d'Utrecht – a vu disparaître la culture de cette plante aromatique et Joop ne partage sa modeste demeure qu'avec son perroquet Gerrit, un animal sexagénaire, bavard et gourmand. Excepté un couple de colombes, il n'y a pas d'autres oiseaux dans la maison. Toutefois, dans l'entrée, dans le salon d'été, dans l'orangerie et dans la cuisine, d'innombrables cages anciennes – vides – trahissent l'affection du maître de maison pour ses «petits amis ailés». En dehors des cages de toutes tailles, Joop collectionne aussi tout ce qui touche au bon vieux temps de nos aïeux. Sa cuisine au carrelage blanc, bourrée de meubles et d'ustensiles anciens aurait pu être le domaine d'une adorable grand-mère aux cheveux blancs et en tablier à carreaux passant des heures à confectionner de délicieux gâteaux secs à la cannelle! Même les couleurs de la maison – bleus délavés, «sang de bœuf» et vert tilleul –, nous parlent d'un «passé définitif». Dans le jardin orné de parterres en buis taillé, une boule de verre, dorée au mercure – de celles qu'on nomme «boules de sorcières» – est censée chasser tout ce qui pourrait nuire au bonheur et troubler l'ambiance paisible de la maison.

Vor dem Haus zeichnen sich die Silhouetten von zwei Lindenbäumen ab, die wie Spalierobst beschnitten sind – eine alte Tradition der Holländer.

Two espaliered lime trees stand in front of the house. This is a very ancient Dutch tradition.

Devant la maison se dressent les silhouettes de deux tilleuls taillés en espalier, une très vieille tradition hollandaise.

Die Delfter Kacheln
mit spielenden Kindern
unterbrechen die
Gleichförmigkeit der
mit »witjes« gekachelten
Wände in der Küche.
Joop ist besonders stolz
auf seine Sammlung
von Kuchenformen aus
glasiertem Ton.

Delft tiles of children at
play break the monot-
ony of the "witje"-
covered kitchen walls.
Joop is inordinately
proud of his collection
of enamelled earthen-
ware cake moulds.

Dans la cuisine, les pe-
tits carreaux en Delft
représentant des «Jeux
d'enfants» animent la
monotonie des murs
recouverts de «witjes».
Joop est particulière-
ment fier de sa collec-
tion de moules à gâ-
teaux en terre émaillée.

INEKE EN ED SCHOKKER

Gelderland

Die Trauerweide und der romantisch verwilderte Garten waren schon vorhanden, aber das alte Bauernhaus bot vor einigen Jahren längst nicht so einen hübschen Anblick wie heute. Seinen besonderen Charme verdankt das Gebäude der Fassade, die mit einer Reihe von Ankern verziert ist, die auf das Entstehungsdatum – 1849 – hinweisen. Die Restaurierung nahmen der Bankier Ed Schokker und seine Frau Ineke vor, die ihr neues Heim mit sensibler Hand von oben bis unten gestaltet und erneuert haben. Dabei waren sie sich stets der Tatsache bewusst, dass es sich bei dem Gebäude um ein besonders schönes Beispiel ländlicher Architektur handelt. Bauernhöfe mit dem traditionellen typischen Zier- und Nutzgarten werden in Holland zunehmend seltener. Die Schokkers beweisen, dass es sich auch im 21. Jahrhundert mit schlichten traditionellen Interieurs ohne überflüssigen Zierrat gut leben lässt. Das Innere des Hauses steht ganz im Zeichen der Nostalgie: Der Boden, dessen Bohlen in Ochsenblutrot gestrichen sind, sonnenblumengelbe Wände und Küchenschränke mit Glastüren, die prall gefüllt sind mit altem Steingut und Porzellan, harmonieren ohne Weiteres mit allem, was den heutigen Wohnstandard ausmacht.

LINKS: *Durch die hängenden Zweige der alten Trauerweide hindurch erkennt man die Eingangstür.*
OBEN: *Das Vogelhaus an dem alten Baum zieht jedes Jahr wieder Vögel an.*

LEFT: *the front door, seen through a veil of weeping willow.*
ABOVE: *A nesting box on an old tree: every year, birds breed in it.*

A GAUCHE: *A travers la cascade de branches d'un vieux saule pleureur, on distingue la porte d'entrée.*
CI-DESSUS: *Un couvoir suspendu à un vieil arbre attire tous les ans un grand nombre d'oiseaux.*

The weeping willow was there already, as was the overgrown garden, but otherwise the old farm had nothing of the freshness we see in it today. Indeed its only claim to fame before it was restored was an unusual facade adorned with a row of anchors proclaiming that it was built in 1849. The couple responsible for this highly successful job of resurrection are a banker, Ed Schokker, and his wife Ineke. They can pride themselves in having renovated their house from top to bottom with exceptional delicacy – and in having never lost sight of the fact that the object of their work was a particularly fine example of Dutch rural architecture. Authentic farms whose gardens have continued to serve as both vegetable patch and "jardin d'agrément" are becoming a rarity in Holland, and the example of the Schokkers teaches us that the 21st century goes very well with the spare, unadorned interiors of Holland's past. Indeed their traditional décor – floorboards painted red, walls painted sunflower yellow and glass-fronted kitchen cabinets crammed with old china and earthenware – can co-exist in total harmony with everything that belongs to modern life.

Eine rote Ziegelstein-fassade und Rasen-flächen mit Buchs-baumkugeln: Die Schokkers haben sich für alte ländliche Traditionen entschieden.

The Schokkers cleave to time-honoured country traditions, with a red brick façade, and grass "parterres" studded with clipped box.

Façade en briques rouges et pelouses ornées de buis taillés en boule: Les Schokker on opté pour les vieilles traditions campagnardes.

Le saule pleureur y était déjà, le jardin abandonné aussi, mais l'ancienne ferme avec sa façade ornée d'une rangée d'ancres qui révèlent l'année de sa construction – 1849 – n'avait pas encore l'aspect pimpant qu'on lui connaît aujourd'hui. Les responsables de cette restauration réussie, le banquier Ed Schokker et sa femme Ineke, se félicitent d'avoir rénové leur acquisition de fond en comble par touches délicates sans perdre de vue qu'il s'agissait ici d'un très bel exemple d'architecture rurale. Les fermes authentiques dont les jardins typiques servent depuis toujours de jardin potager et de jardin d'agrément, se font de plus en plus rares aux Pays-Bas. Et l'exemple des Schokker nous apprend aussi que le 21ᵉ siècle s'intègre parfaitement dans ces intérieurs nostalgiques dépouillés de tout ornement superflu. Leurs décors traditionnels de planchers peints couleur sang de bœuf, de murs jaune tournesol et d'armoires de cuisine vitrées où sont accumulées des faïences et des porcelaines anciennes peuvent coexister harmonieusement avec tout ce qui touche à notre mode de vie actuel.

Der hellrosa Rosenbusch ragt aus einem Hosta-beet empor.

Bright pink roses bursting from a bed planted with hostas.

Le rose vif d'un buisson de roses émerge d'un massif de hostas.

OBEN UND RECHTE
SEITE: *Ed hat den
Geräteschuppen, der
gleichzeitig als Garage
dient, entworfen und
gebaut. Hier bewahrt
Ineke ihre alten Blu-
mentöpfe und ihre Gar-
tengeräte auf, im Som-
mer jedoch nutzt sie
den Schuppen auch als
Gartenpavillon.*
RECHTS: *ein schmie-
deeiserner Türstopper
in Form einer wohl-
genährten Milchkuh …*

ABOVE AND FACING
PAGE: *The toolshed-
garage was designed
and built by Ed him-
self. Here Ineke stores
her old terracotta pots
and garden tools; she
also uses it as a summer
house.*
RIGHT: *a cast-iron
doorstopper in the form
of a fat milch cow.*

CI-DESSUS ET PAGE
DE DROITE: *C'est
Ed qui a dessiné et
construit la grange à
outils qui sert aussi de
garage. Ineke y range ses
vieux pots en terre cuite
et ses outils de jardi-
nage, mais la grange
fait aussi office de pa-
villon d'été.*
A DROITE: *Un arrêt-
de-porte en fonte a pris
la forme d'une vache à
lait bien nourrie.*

LINKS: *Der große eingebaute Vitrinenschrank ziert mit seinem wertvollen Inhalt – Steingut und blauweißes Geschirr – die Küche.*
RECHTE SEITE: *In der Küche haben sich die Schokkers für Gartenmöbel aus Holz und Schmiedeeisen entschieden.*

LEFT: *a substantial glass-fronted dresser in the kitchen filled with fine crockery – notably Creamware and a blue-and-white service.*
FACING PAGE: *The Schokkers have imported wooden and wrought-iron garden furniture into the kitchen.*

A GAUCHE: *Le contenu précieux du grand vaisselier encastré égaye la cuisine. Ses éléments principaux sont un service «Cream-ware» et une vaisselle bleue et blanche.*
PAGE DE DROITE: *Les Schokker n'ont pas hésité à introduire des meubles de jardin en bois et fer forgé dans la cuisine.*

RECHTS: *Das Sonnenlicht fällt auf die strohgelben Stufen und Geländer der Treppe. Die schmiedeeiserne Lampe ist die Kopie eines antiken Modells.*

RIGHT: *The sunlit staircase and banisters are painted butter-yellow. The wrought-iron lantern was copied from an antique original.*

A DROITE: *La cage d'escalier et la balustrade peintes d'une couleur «beurre» accrochent la lumière. La lanterne en fer forgé est la copie d'un modèle ancien.*

LINKS: *Die modernen Elemente der Küche beeinträchtigen keineswegs die authentische Stimmung des Raumes. Die Abzugshaube und die Schranktüren wurden Feuerwehr-Rot lackiert.*

RECHTE SEITE: *Auf einem Gartentisch mit farbigen, in Zement eingebetteten Mosaikfliesen serviert Ineke ihr Lieblingsgetränk Tee. Dazu reicht sie köstliche »stroopwafels«, Sirupwaffeln.*

LEFT: *The contemporary elements in the kitchen don't detract in any way from the authentic ambience. The stove-hood and the shelves are painted fire engine red.*

FACING PAGE: *Ineke serves tea on a garden table encrusted with brightly-coloured cement tiles. The fare includes an assortment of delicious "stroopwafels" – waffles with treacle.*

A GAUCHE: *Les éléments contemporains de la cuisine ne troublent nullement l'ambiance authentique des lieux. La hotte et les rangements ont été peints en rouge «sapeur pompier».*

PAGE DE DROITE: *Sur une table de jardin incrustée de dalles en ciment aux vifs coloris, Ineke sert le thé et accompagne sa boisson favorite d'un assortiment de «stroopwafels» – des gaufrettes au sirop – absolument délicieuses.*

EN KASTEEL IN DE BETUWE
Barbara en René Stoeltie

De Betuwe

Wenn wir zurückdenken, scheint es, als ob nicht wir es waren, die dieses Schloss aus dem 17. Jahrhundert im Herzen der Region Betuwe entdeckt haben. Vielmehr hat das robuste strenge Gebäude, umgeben von einem Wassergraben und einem englischen Park, seit langem auf uns gewartet. Wenn wir heute Bilanz ziehen, müssen wir zugeben, dass wir bei der Neudekoration die weitläufigen Räume mit den Originalvertäfelungen nicht gerade geschont haben. Unser Vorhaben, die romantische Atmosphäre des 18. Jahrhunderts wiederherzustellen, war mit einigem Aufwand verbunden, auch wenn es uns viel Freude bereitet hat. Wir suchten nach solchen Möbeln, Stoffen, Tapeten und Familienporträts, die alten Gebäuden erst eine Seele geben, und haben auf Reisen durch die ganze Welt nach Inspirationen für die Einrichtung gesucht. Beeinflusst haben uns Aufenthalte in zahlreichen Schlössern in Frankreich, England, Deutschland und Schweden: Aus einem haben wir das herrliche Muster der Wände übernommen, aus einem anderen die harmonischen Grau-, Blau- und Gelbtöne abgeschaut. Und so strahlt das Gebäude genau die lässige Eleganz aus, die das Leben auf dem Schloss auszeichnet. Mitten in der Betuwe, umgeben von jahrhundertealten Bäumen und einer Landschaft wie in einem Gemälde von Jacob van Ruisdael, lässt es sich gut leben …

LINKS: *Ein mit Raureif überzogenes Spinnennetz umgarnt den Widder, der eine der Urnen auf dem Schlossplatz ziert.*
OBEN: *Der Pfeil der Sonnenuhr auf dem Steinsockel zielt in den Himmel.*

LEFT: *A spider's web covered in rime hangs from a ram's head on one of the urns in the castle forecourt.*
ABOVE: *A sundial on a stone plinth points its arrow skywards.*

A GAUCHE: *Une toile d'araignée couverte de givre s'accroche à la tête de bélier qui orne l'une des urnes du parvis.*
CI-DESSUS: *Un cadran solaire monté sur un socle en pierre pointe sa flèche vers le ciel.*

Looking back, it is quite possible that it wasn't a case of our discovering this 17th-century castle in the heart of the Betuwe, but rather that the building itself, with its moats and English park, had been awaiting our coming for many, many years. When we take stock of the way we changed the décor, we realise that we didn't exactly spare these broad, panelled rooms. Indeed our desire to recreate the romantic ambience of the 18th-century, to find the furniture, the fabrics, the wallpapers and family portraits that are the life and soul of such ancestral homes required a real effort, fun though it was. Being much influenced by our travels around the world and by our visits to scores of similar buildings in France, England, Germany and Sweden, we borrowed from one of them the beautiful design of our wallpaper and from another the cameo greys, blues and lemon yellows which form our daily surroundings. From all of them in some measure we stole the relaxed elegance which is the hallmark of what the French call "la vie de chateau". And in the heart of the Betuwe, surrounded by old trees and a landscape straight from a painting by Jacob van Ruisdael, that kind of life is well worth living.

Vom Schlossplatz aus betrachtet erinnert das Gebäude mit den jahrhundertealten Linden an ein Gemälde von Caspar David Friedrich.

Seen from the forecourt, the castle stands behind its screen of old lime-trees like a dream-image from Caspar David Friedrich.

Vu du parvis, le château, entouré de vieux tilleuls, semble sorti d'un tableau de Caspar David Friedrich.

Avec le recul, nous nous disons souvent que nous n'avons peut-être pas découvert ce château du 17ᵉ au cœur de la Betuwe. En fait, on dirait plutôt que ce bâtiment robuste et sévère, entouré de douves et d'un parc à l'anglaise nous attendait depuis longtemps … Faisant le bilan de notre «changement de décor»: avouons sans détours que nous n'avons pas épargné ces vastes salons tapissés de lambris d'époque et que notre désir de recréer l'ambiance romantique du 18ᵉ siècle, de trouver le mobilier, les tissus, les papiers peints et les portraits de famille qui sont l'âme des vieilles demeures ancestrales fut un effort enchanteur. Influencés par nos voyages à travers le monde et par nos séjours dans un grand nombre de châteaux en France, en Angleterre, en Allemagne et en Suède, nous avons emprunté à l'un ces ravissantes indiennes à fleurs qui couvrent nos murs, escamoté à l'autre les camaïeux de gris, de bleu et de jaune citron qui forment notre décor quotidien et carrément «dérobé» à tous cette élégance décontractée qui est le propre de «la vie de château». Au cœur de la Betuwe, entourés d'arbres séculaires et d'un paysage à la Ruisdael, la vie vaut la peine d'être vécue.

Das Schloss in Morgennebel gehüllt.

The castle through the morning mist.

Le château enveloppé d'un brouillard matinal.

OBEN UND RECHTE
SEITE: *Das Esszimmer
im Louis-Seize-Stil hat
alles, um Liebhaber des
nordischen Stils zu be-
geistern: indisch ange-
hauchte Vertäfelungen
in Blau und Weiß, einen
Lüster aus dem 18. Jahr-
hundert und die Porzel-
lanskulptur »Cupido
schärft seinen Pfeil«.*
RECHTS: *Der Juno-
Kopf aus dem 19. Jahr-
hundert wurde auf ei-
nem Directoire-Tisch
platziert.*
FOLGENDE DOPPEL-
SEITE: *ein Medaillon
mit einem Porträt von
Friedrich Schiller und
das Bildnis von Gillart
de Lachantel.*

ABOVE AND FACING
PAGE: *The dining
room is austere and
elegant in the style of
Louis Seize, with panels
covered in a blue and
white fabric with an
Indian design. An 18th-
century chandelier
hangs above the table,
over a piece of Sèvres
china representing
"Cupid sharpening his
arrow".*
RIGHT: *A 19th-century
head of Juno stands on
a Directoire table.*
FOLLOWING PAGES:
*a medallion of
Friedrich Schiller and
the portrait of Gillart
de Lachantel.*

CI-DESSUS ET PAGE
DE DROITE: *La salle à
manger de style Louis
Seize dont les lambris
sont habillés d'une
«indienne» bleue et
blanche, a tout pour
charmer les amoureux
d'un style nordique
sévère et élégant. Le
lustre est 18ᵉ, et le
groupe en Sèvres repré-
sente «Cupidon aigui-
sant sa flèche».*
A DROITE: *Une tête
de Junon 19ᵉ est posée
sur une table Direc-
toire.*
DOUBLE PAGE SUI-
VANTE: *un médaillon
représentant Friedrich
Schiller et le portrait de
Gillart de Lachantel.*

Der Salon wurde in der Tradition des 18. Jahrhunderts eingerichtet: ein Ruhebett mit einem »Polonaise«-Himmel, Louis-Quinze- und Louis-Seize-Möbel sowie eine Tapete mit einem Muster, das an chinesische Malerei erinnert.

The salon is decorated in the grand tradition of the 18th-century: daybed draped "à la polonaise", period Louis-Quinze and Louis-Seize furniture and wallpaper inspired by Chinese paintings.

Le salon a été décoré dans la grande tradition 18e : lit de repos drapé «à la polonaise», mobilier d'époque Louis Quinze et Louis Seize et papier peint inspiré par les peintures chinoises.

HET KOETSHUIS

Martine Ambtman en Dicky Vos

Gelderland

Hinter einer Gruppe jahrhundertealter Bäume verbirgt sich das
große Haus aus dem 19. Jahrhundert, über dessen Eingangstür
sich ein Halbmond aus vergoldetem Metall im Wind wiegt. »Het
Koetshuis«, das Kutscherhaus, verdankt seinen Namen der alten
Remise, die sich an das stattliche Haupthaus schmiegt. Martine
Ambtman und Dicky Vos, die das Haus dem Dorfpfarrer abgekauft
haben, um sich hier mit ihrem Antiquitätengeschäft und ihrer viel-
köpfigen Familie niederzulassen, haben vor allem die Lage und der
gute Zustand des Gebäudes überzeugt. Martine und Dicky haben
ein Faible für alles Ländliche und erwarben mit »Het Koetshuis«
ein neues Heim, das endlich auch den passenden Rahmen für ihre
große Sammlung an Möbeln, Geschirr, Wäsche und rustikalen
Küchengeräten bot. Die vielen Deckenbalken, alten Kamine, Mauern und Vertäfelungen, die noch immer die Originalfarbe aufwei-
sen, verleihen dem Haus einen unerwarteten Charme und so geriet
die Neudekoration zu einem subtilen Spiel von Illusion und opti-
scher Täuschung. Zu Beginn eines neuen Jahrtausends, voller kalter
und unpersönlicher Technologie, begeistert das nostalgische Flair
der alten Remise ganz besonders.

LINKS: *Die Apfelernte
im Obstgarten war er-
giebig.*
OBEN: *eine Symphonie
aus Primärfarben,
komponiert aus dem
Rot des Schrankes, der
blauen Kanne und dem
gelben Becher.*

LEFT: *a rich harvest of
apples from the orchard.*
ABOVE: *a symphony of
primary colours – red
wardrobe, blue pitcher,
yellow goblet.*

A GAUCHE: *une belle
récolte de pommes
cueillies dans le verger.*
CI-DESSUS: *une sym-
phonie de couleurs pri-
maires composée d'une
armoire rouge, d'une
verseuse bleue et d'un
gobelet jaune.*

The rambling 19th-century house lies hidden behind a row of ancient trees and the sign over the gate – a crescent moon in gilded metal – swings gently in the wind. "Het Koetshuis" – The Carriage House – is an old building backing on to a large gentleman's residence, but Martine Ambtman and Dicky Vos, who bought the place from the village parson with a view to setting up an antique shop and raising a large family under its roof, claim that the things they liked best about it were its site and the fact that it was fully intact. Martine and Dicky love everything to do with country life, and when they bought "Het Koetshuis" they were able – finally – to display their full array of country furniture, earthenware, household linen and cooking utensils. Since the house also offered the undreamt-of luxury of a décor rich in old beams and fireplaces, with walls and panels still bearing their original paintwork, their decoration work became a subtle game of optical illusion. At the dawn of a new millennium, with mankind threatened by its own cold technology, the nostalgic interiors of "Het Koetshuis" still have the power to enchant us.

Es gibt nichts Holländisches als ein »Velo« im Stil der 1930er-Jahre, das nonchalant am Zaun eines Landhauses lehnt.

A 1930s style bicycle leaning nonchalantly against the railings of a house in the country – the vignette could hardly be more Dutch.

Quoi de plus hollandais qu'un «vélo» style années 1930 posé non-chalamment contre la clôture d'une maison de campagne?

Die Bewohner haben sich einen kleinen Platz an der Sonne reserviert. Der gusseiserne Gartenstuhl an der Eingangstür ist ein Entwurf von Karl Friedrich Schinkel.

The inmates have fashioned themselves a place in the sun; the cast-iron garden chair by the door is by Karl Friedrich Schinkel.

Les habitants se sont réservé une petite place au soleil. La chaise de jardin en fonte près de la porte d'entrée est signée Karl Friedrich Schinkel.

La grande maison 19ᵉ est cachée derrière une rangée d'arbres séculaires et l'enseigne au-dessus de la porte – un croissant de lune en métal doré – se berce au gré du vent. «Het Koetshuis», la Remise à carrosses, a emprunté son nom à l'ancienne remise adossée au flanc de cette robuste maison de maître. Martine Ambtman et Dicky Vos, qui ont acheté la propriété au curé du village afin d'y installer leur magasin d'antiquités et d'abriter leur famille nombreuse, prétendent qu'avant tout elles ont été séduites par le site et par l'aspect intact du bâtiment. Martine et Dicky adorent tout ce qui touche à la vie à la campagne et l'acquisition de «Het Koetshuis» leur donne enfin la possibilité de mettre en scène leur vaste collection de meubles, de faïences, de linge de maison et d'ustensiles de cuisine rustiques. Comme leur nouveau gîte offrait le luxe inespéré d'un décor riche en poutres apparentes et en vieilles cheminées et que les murs et les boiseries étaient toujours recouverts de la peinture d'origine, leur effort en matière de décoration devint un jeu subtil de supercheries et d'illusions optiques. A l'aube d'un nouveau millénaire menacé par une technologie froide et inhumaine, les intérieurs nostalgiques de l'ancienne remise continuent de nous enchanter.

LINKS: *Im Wohnzimmer bilden ein massiver Tisch, Stühle mit Strohgeflecht und eine Bank, auf der man sich früher am Kamin wärmte, eine einladende Essecke. Der rustikale Geschirrschrank stammt aus Mitteleuropa, genau wie die Teller aus glasiertem Ton.*
RECHTE SEITE: *In diesen milden Septembertagen kann man noch gut draußen essen.*

LEFT: *In the living room, a sturdy table, straw-bottomed chairs and a bench which used to be by the fireplace. The rustic dresser comes from Central Europe, as do the enamelled earthenware plates.*
FACING PAGE: *On mild September days one can still eat outside.*

A GAUCHE: *Dans le séjour, une robuste table, des chaises paillées et une banquette qui servait jadis à se réchauffer près de la cheminée forment un coin-repas accueillant. Le vaisselier rustique est originaire d'Europe centrale ainsi que les plats en terre émaillée.*
PAGE DE DROITE: *Le doux mois de septembre est propice aux repas en plein air.*

Einer der schönsten
Räume ist die große
Küche. Da Martine
und Dicky leidenschaft-
lich gerne backen, fin-
den sich auf dem Tisch
alle Küchengeräte und
Zutaten, die man für
einen köstlichen Sand-
kuchen benötigt.

The spacious kitchen
is one of the most wel-
coming places in the
house. Martine and
Dicky are ace cake
makers, and the ingre-
dients for a delicious
"sablé" pastry are laid
out on the table.

La grande cuisine est
un des endroits les plus
sympathiques de la
maison. Martine et
Dicky adorent faire de
la pâtisserie: la farine
répandue et les moules,
plats et ustensiles divers
sur la table annoncent
la confection d'une déli-
cieuse pâte sablée.

$\mathcal{H}$UIS TE HURWENEN
Mynke Buskens en Andreas von Bertleff
Gelderland

Das große quadratische Haus wird zur Hälfte von herrlichen alten Linden veredelt. Robust und prächtig erhebt es sich auf dem Deich und man versteht sofort, weshalb die Zeichnerin Mynke Buskens und ihr Partner Andreas von Bertleff, ein Mosaikexperte, beschlossen haben, sich in diesem kleinen Ort mit dem ungewöhnlichen Namen Hurwenen niederzulassen. »Huis te Hurwenen«, das Haus von Hurwenen, wurde in der Blüte der viktorianischen Epoche erbaut. Typisch für diese Ära, die sich ebenso durch Prüderie wie Größenwahn auszeichnet, sind die zum Teil überdimensionalen Proportionen, die marmornen Kamine im Rokokostil, das schöne Kupferwaschbecken in Muschelform, die geschwungene Wendeltreppe und der riesige Speicher, in dem Mynke sofort ihr Atelier einrichtete. Ihre großformatigen Kohlezeichnungen von imaginären Tunneln, Parkanlagen und Städten kommen in diesem Umfeld gut zur Geltung. Und im großen Salon hat Mynke ihre Werke – Größenwahn verpflichtet – kühn zu Wandverkleidungen umfunktioniert; die schlichten dunklen Möbel lenken von den Bildern nicht ab. Nur das Bad, das ganz mit Bronze- und Goldmosaiken verkleidet ist, zeugt von einem unwiederstehlichen Hang zum Luxus.

Ein Steinornament ruht auf der Fensterbank.

A stone ornament on the windowsill.

Un ornement en pierre repose sur l'appui de fenêtre.

The house stands foursquare, partly obscured by a screen of magnificent lime trees. It dominates the dyke on which it stands, and you immediately understand why the designer Mynke Buskens and her partner Andreas von Bertleff, who is an expert on mosaics, have chosen to live in this oddly-named village of Hurwenen. "Huis te Hurwenen", or Hurwenen House, was built at the height of the prudish and megalomaniac Victorian era. It is typically out of proportion, with rocaille marble fireplaces, pretty shell-shaped brass washbasins, a spiral staircase and a huge attic in which Mynke has set up her studio. Her work, which consists of huge charcoal drawings of imaginary parks and cities, looks particularly well in this outsize environment. In the main drawing room, she has had the audacity – megalomaniac obliged – to transform her drawings into panels. From a decorating point of view the sobriety of the dark wooden furniture does not clash with the artwork and only the bathroom, all covered in bronze and gold mosaics, gives any hint of the couple's irrepressible love of luxury.

Mynke meditiert vor einer Kiste – einem ihrer Kunstwerke.

Mynke contemplates a box – a work of art of her own creation.

Mynke médite devant une boîte – un objet d'art de sa création.

»Huis te Hurwenen« liegt hinter den grünen Zweigen hundertjähriger Bäume verborgen.

"Huis te Hurwenen" is hidden behind a veil of greenery formed by the tops of ancient trees.

«Huis te Hurwenen», derrière un écran de verdure formé par les cimes touffues des arbres centenaires.

La grande maison carrée, à moitié dissimulée par un écran de vieux tilleuls superbes, domine la digue de toute sa splendeur robuste et on comprend tout de suite pourquoi Mynke Buskens, dessinatrice de talent, et son partenaire Andreas von Bertleff, expert en mosaïque, ont choisi de s'installer dans ce petit village au nom singulier de Hurwenen. Le «Huis te Hurwenen», la maison de Hurwenen, a été bâti en pleine époque victorienne et, de cette ère aussi prude que mégalomane, il a hérité ses proportions souvent inégales, ses cheminées en marbre de style rocaille, sa jolie fontaine murale de cuivre en forme de coquille, son escalier en colimaçon et l'immense grenier où Mynke a tout de suite installé son atelier. Ses dessins au fusain représentant des passages souterrains, des parcs et des cités imaginaires ont trouvé un décor digne de leur format hors normes. Dans le grand salon, Mynke – mégalomanie oblige – a même eu l'audace de les transformer en lambris. Côté décoration, la sobriété des meubles en bois sombre ne fait pas concurrence aux œuvres d'art. Seule la salle de bains, toute en mosaïques bronze et or, témoigne d'un penchant irrépressible pour le luxe.

LINKE SEITE: *Auf einem Tisch hat Mynke Kohlekreiden, Bürsten, Stifte und Radiergummis ausgebreitet.*
OBEN: *Der weitläufige Speicher dient heute als Atelier.*
RECHTS: *An den Wänden im Esszimmer hängen Zeichnungen, die den unterirdischen Fluss Binnen-Dieze zeigen.*
FOLGENDE DOPPEL-SEITE: *Die Treppe führt zum Aussichtspunkt auf dem Dach. Das Waschbecken aus Gusseisen und Kupfer gehörte schon immer zur Ausstattung.*

FACING PAGE: *Mynke's charcoals, brushes, pencils and erasers, blackened by constant use.*
ABOVE: *The attic is now a studio.*
RIGHT: *In the dining room the walls are covered by a series of drawings representing the tunnels of the Binnen-Dieze, an underground river.*
FOLLOWING PAGES: *The staircase leads up to a belvedere on the roof. The brass and cast-iron washbasin have been there from the beginning.*

PAGE DE GAUCHE: *Sur une table, Mynke a étalé ses fusains, ses brosses, ses crayons et ses gommes.*
CI-DESSUS: *L'ancien grenier est devenu l'atelier.*
A DROITE: *Les murs de la salle à manger sont recouverts de dessins qui représentent les tunnels de la Binnen-Dieze, une rivière souterraine.*
DOUBLE PAGE SUIVANTE: *L'escalier mène au belvédère sur le toit. La fontaine murale en cuivre et en fonte a vu le jour avec la maison.*

ISCHA VAN DELFT EN JACQUES MASSÉ

Gelderland

Es muss einigen Mut erfordert haben, sich auf das verfallene, nur wenige Meter von der Maas entfernte, alte Café einzulassen, aber die neuen Inhaber Ischa van Delft und Jacques Massé waren risikofreudig genug, es zu kaufen. Die Dekorateurin Ischa schätzt die Romantik des Landlebens sehr und sie wusste beim ersten Anblick, dass es ihr gelingen würde, dieses Labyrinth von Räumen mit undankbaren Proportionen in ein einladendes, gemütliches Haus zu verwandeln. Im Vertrauen auf ihren Partner, der eine Vorliebe für skandinavische Möbel aus dem 18. Jahrhundert, den amerikanischen Kolonialstil und alte Patina hat, machte sie sich an die Arbeit. Heute erinnert nichts mehr an den heruntergekommenen Gastraum, in dem sich früher die Bauern aus der Umgebung ein Gläschen Genever genehmigten. Van Delft und Massé erweiterten das ehemalige Café um ein blau-grün vertäfeltes Esszimmer und eine knallrot getünchte Küche, in der sich die Familie und Freunde auf einen Kaffee oder ein leckeres Essen treffen. Die Hausherrin ist besonders stolz auf ihre jüngstes Werk: einen Garten, in dem der Blick über zahllose Rosen, eine Wasserfläche und ein kleines Häuschen gleitet, in dessen Schutz man Mahlzeiten »im Freien« einnehmen kann.

LINKS: *Ein Strauß rosa Pfingstrosen wurde auf dem Sims eines Schranks platziert, der mit antiken Gläsern gefüllt ist.*
OBEN: *Ischa kann aus wenigen Zweigen ein faszinierendes Arrangement gestalten.*

LEFT: *a bouquet of pink peonies left on the edge of a dresser filled with old glass.*
ABOVE: *Ischa has the gift of transforming a few cut branches into an eye-catching flower arrangement.*

A GAUCHE: *Un bouquet de pivoines roses posé sur le rebord d'une armoire remplie de verreries anciennes.*
CI-DESSUS: *Ischa sait transformer quelques branches coupées en bouquet surprenant.*

Die Fassade des An-
baus, der früher als
Raststätte diente.

The façade of the an-
nexe that was once a
restaurant.

La façade de l'ancien
café-relais routier.

A certain kind of courage was needed to tackle this old bro-
ken-down café beside the River Meuse, but Ischa van Delft
and Jacques Massé had what it took, in spades. Ischa is a decorator whose special passion is romantic country life – and
from the moment she laid eyes on this labyrinth of awk-
wardly-shaped rooms she knew she was equal to the task of
transforming them into a warm and welcoming place to live.
Moreover she could rely on the unequivocal support of a partner who swears by 18th-century Scandinavian furniture, the
American colonial style and the authentic patinas of age. So
that was all right, too. If you go to the café now, you won't
find the vaguest hint of the original pumproom with its bat-
tered bar, where the local farmers once came to quaff their
shotglasses of "genever". In its stead Van Delft and Massé have
concocted a dining room with blue-green panelled walls and
a kitchen painted bright red, where their family and friends
foregather to take coffee or enjoy the succulent meals prepared
by the mistress of the house. But Ischa herself is altogether
proudest of her most recent creation – a garden in which the
eye lingers on seas of old roses, a rectangular pond, and a folly
at the far end where she can take her meals "al fresco".

Il fallait du courage pour s'attaquer à ce vieux café délabré situé à quelques pas de la Meuse, mais du courage, les nouveaux
propriétaires Ischa van Delft et Jacques Massé en avaient à revendre … Ischa, une décoratrice que passionne le romantisme
de la vie campagnarde a su dès le premier coup d'œil qu'elle
réussirait à transformer ce labyrinthe aux volumes ingrats en
une maison chaleureuse et accueillante. Se sachant secondée
par un partenaire qui vénère les meubles scandinaves d'époque
18e, le style colonial américain et les patines à l'ancienne, elle
s'est mise au travail. De nos jours, rien ne rappelle l'ancienne
salle commune au zinc fatigué où les paysans des alentours ve-
naient prendre leur petit verre de genièvre. Grâce à van Delft
et Massé, l'ancien bistrot s'est enrichi d'une salle à manger aux
lambris bleu vert et d'une cuisine aux murs badigeonnés d'un
rouge vif où la famille et les amis se réunissent pour prendre
un café ou pour goûter aux petits plats mijotés par la maîtresse
de maison. Celle-ci se montre toujours fière de sa dernière
création: un jardin où l'œil s'attarde sur des massifs de roses
anciennes, un plan d'eau et un abri rustique pour les repas en
plein air.

Die Hündin Tess ist in
ihrer schattigen Nische
unter einem Regal ein-
geschlummert.

Ischa's dog Tess, in her
bed under a shelf.

La chienne Tess s'est en-
dormie dans sa niche à
l'ombre d'une étagère.

RECHTS: *Dieser große Raum ist Jacques' persönliches Refugium. Hier hortet er seine Fundstücke, hier hat er sich aus Möbeln und Vertäfelungen, die schon Patina angesetzt haben, sein eigenes Paradies geschaffen.*
FOLGENDE DOPPELSEITE: *Nautische Geräte, Türen und Vertäfelungen, von denen die Farbe abblättert, ein Holzpferd, von einem Trödler aus Neuengland … Jacques kann mit allem etwas anfangen.*

RIGHT: *This spacious room with its old panelling is the exclusive domain of Jacques, full of his personal treasures, rare objects and furniture.*
FOLLOWING PAGES: *Nautical objects, doors and panels covered in peeling paint, a wooden horse found in a New England junkshop … no matter what, Jacques has a way of making the best use of things.*

A DROITE: *Cette grande pièce est le domaine exclusif de Jacques. C'est ici qu'il expose ses trouvailles et qu'il a créé son paradis personnel avec des objets rares et des meubles et des lambris patinés par le temps.*
DOUBLE PAGE SUIVANTE: *Objets nautiques, portes et lambris recouverts de peinture écaillée, un cheval de bois déniché dans une brocante de Nouvelle-Angleterre. Peu importe … Jacques sait toujours en tirer le meilleur parti.*

OBEN: *In ihrer Küche hat Ischa roten Putz für die Wände und billard-grüne Farbe für Tür und Fensterrahmen gewählt.*

RECHTS: *Auf der Toilette bilden ein antikes Waschbecken, ein Gartenstuhl und der rote Ziegelsteinboden ein schönes Still-Leben.*

RECHTE SEITE: *Eine Tür aus dem 18. Jahrhundert, die Jacques aus Frankreich mitgebracht hat, fand in dem Gartenhäuschen ihr neues Zuhause.*

ABOVE: *In her kitchen, Ischa has covered the stucco walls with a red wash; the door and its casing are painted billiard-baize green.*

RIGHT: *An old washbasin, a garden seat and a floor in red brick make an unexpected combination for the cloakroom.*

FACING PAGE: *An 18th-century door, which Jacques brought home from France, has found a place in the garden shed.*

CI-DESSUS: *Ischa a choisi de couvrir d'un lavis rouge les murs en stuc de sa cuisine et de peindre la porte et le chambranle en vert billard.*

A DROITE: *Dans les toilettes, un lave-mains ancien, un siège de jardin et un sol en briques rouges forment un ensemble inattendu.*

PAGE DE DROITE: *Une porte 18ᵉ, que Jacques a rapportée de France, a trouvé son emplacement définitif dans l'abri de jardin.*

EEN TUINHUISJE
Ischa van Delft en Jacques Massé
Gelderland

Ursprünglich gab es nur ein unbebautes Gelände hinter einem großen Haus aus der Jahrhundertwende. Ischa van Delft und Jacques Massé hatten sich der schwierigen Aufgabe gestellt, das unfruchtbare Land in einen traumhaften Garten mit Pavillon im Stil des 18. Jahrhunderts zu verwandeln. Zwar gab es durchaus Momente des Zweifels und der Mutlosigkeit, aber das Paar Van Delft-Massé ließ sich nicht unterkriegen; und wenn man heute durch das Fotoalbum vom Umbau blättert, muss man unwillkürlich lächeln. Es gibt Bilder von Jacques, wie er im Schlamm watet oder Bretter und Vertäfelungen schleppt, und auch Aufnahmen von der erschöpften Ischa, die Bäume und Kletterrosen pflanzt oder die Teerpappe auf dem Dach einschneidet, um der Dachkante die Wirkung einer romantischen Girlande zu verleihen. Heute kann man sich gar nicht mehr vorstellen, welche Anstrengungen mit dem Bau einer Wand mit Portikus und Vasen aus gedrechseltem Holz verbunden sind. Schwer vorstellbar ist auch, dass dort, wo heute Blumenbeete und Rosen in zarten Farben strahlen, früher absolute Einöde war und dass der »barocke« Pavillon mit dem sonnenblumengelben Interieur, der eingebauten Bettnische, dem gusseisernen Ofen und den karierten Vorhängen in Wirklichkeit Ende des 20. Jahrhunderts entstanden ist.

In the beginning, there was nothing here but a piece of waste-
land behind the large turn-of-the-century house occupied by
Ischa van Delft and Jacques Massé. Later the couple set about
the heavy task of transforming their arid plot into a dreamlike
garden, with a pavilion at its end in the best 18th-century
taste. As the work progressed, they had moments of doubt
and despair. Nevertheless they strove on manfully – and when
you see their photo album you realise just how manful they
had to be. There are pictures of Jacques slogging through the
mud and hauling planks about, while the exhausted Ischa
plants trees and climbing roses or cuts up the tarred material
for the pavilion roof in such a way as to give the eaves the look
of a pelmet. It is impossible, in this day and age, to guess at
the sheer effort that lies behind the construction of a wall em-
bellished by a portico and crowned with wooden vases turned
on a lathe; or even to suspect that where now you see great
masses of delicate roses and other blossoms, there was once
nothing but bare ground. Hardest of all to grasp is the fact
that this 18th-century pavilion with its sunflower yellow interior, its box bed, its cast-iron stove and its chequered curtains,
dates from the last years of the 20th century.

*Unter dem Dachvor-
sprung des »paviljong«
lässt sich das schöne
Wetter genießen.*

*The sunny porch of the
"paviljong".*

*Qu'il fait bon profiter
du beau temps sous
l'auvent du «pavil-
jong».*

Au début ce n'était qu'un terrain vague derrière une grande
maison fin de siècle. Ischa van Delft et Jacques Massé qui ont
entrepris la lourde tâche de transformer cette terre aride en
jardin de rêve et de construire un pavillon, tout au bout de ce
jardin, dans le meilleur goût 18ᵉ, avouent qu'ils ont connu des
moments de doute et de désespoir. Le couple Van Delft-Massé
ne s'est pas découragé pour autant et quand on feuillette l'album photo de la transformation, on a envie de rire car les
images nous montrent Jacques, pataugeant dans la boue ou
traînant des planches et des lambris et nous révèlent Ischa,
épuisée, plantant des arbres et des rosiers grimpants ou décou-
pant la toile goudronnée sur le toit du pavillon afin de donner
au rebord l'aspect d'un lambrequin romantique. Impossible de
nos jours de deviner l'effort que représente la construction
d'un mur orné d'un portique et couronné de vases en bois
tourné, de soupçonner que le vide absolu régnait là où poussent aujourd'hui des massifs de fleurs et de roses aux couleurs
tendres, et que le pavillon «18ᵉ» avec son intérieur jaune tournesol, son lit d'alcôve, son poêle en fonte et ses rideaux à carreaux ne date que de la fin du 20ᵉ siècle.

*Kletterrosen rahmen
den Blick auf die große
Vase, den Teich und das
»tuinhuisje«.*

*Climbing roses frame
the view towards the
urn, the pond and the
"tuinhuisje".*

*Une arche couverte
d'un rosier grimpant
encercle la vue sur le
vase Médicis, le plan
d'eau et le «tuinhuisje».*

Kaum vorstellbar, dass
diese paradiesische Ecke
mal ein tristes graues
Gelände gewesen sein
soll. Die große gussei-
serne Vase am hinteren
Ende des Teichs, die das
Paar in Frankreich auf-
gestöbert hat, stammt
aus dem 19. Jahrhun-
dert.

It's hard to believe that
only a few years ago this
corner of paradise was a
dreary vacant lot. The
tall 19th century vase at
the far end of the pond
came from France.

On a peine à croire
que ce coin de paradis
n'était autrefois qu'un
terrain vague morne et
gris. Le grand vase en
fonte, à l'extrémité de la
pièce d'eau, est 19ᵉ et a
été déniché en France.

OBEN UND RECHTS:
In weniger als zwei Jahren hat Ischa ein dürres Stück Land in einen üppigen Garten verwandelt, in dem ihre Lieblingspflanzen, -bäume und -rosen prächtig gedeihen. Stets risikofreudig, hat sie ihre alten und seltenen Stoffe einfach gewaschen …
RECHTE SEITE: *Der Tisch ist gedeckt und die Mahlzeit kann beginnen.*

ABOVE AND RIGHT:
In less than two years, Ischa transformed this square of arid ground into a luxuriant garden where she can grow her favourite plants, roses and trees. Nor does she balk at washing her rarest and oldest fabrics and hanging them in the sun to dry …
FACING PAGE: *a table set for lunch outside.*

CI-DESSUS ET A DROITE: *En deux ans à peine, Ischa a transformé ce carré de terre aride en un jardin luxuriant où poussent ses plantes, ses arbres et ses roses préférées. Avec l'intrépidité qui la caractérise, elle a couru le risque de laver ses tissus anciens et rares …*
PAGE DE DROITE: *La table est mise et le repas à la fraîche peut commencer.*

LINKS: *Nelken, Veilchen und rot-weiße Papageientulpen fügen sich zu einem bezaubernden Strauß in einer schlichten Glasvase.*
RECHTE SEITE: *Die gesteppte Decke auf dem massiven Tisch im Pavillon wurde nach Ischas Angaben in Indien gefertigt. Sie hat denselben gelb-orangen Farbton für die Wände ausgewählt und die Vorhänge aus einem karierten Stoff genäht, den sie auch in ihrem Laden verkauft.*

LEFT: *Carnations, violets and red-and-white parrot-tulips create a magical effect in a simple glass vase.*
FACING PAGE: *In the pavilion, the quilted cloth draped over the table was made in India to Ischa's specifications. She also selected the yellow-orange shade of the walls and made the curtains from a chequered fabric that she sells in her shop.*

A GAUCHE: *Des œillets, des violettes et des tulipes «perroquet» rouges et blanches forment un bouquet charmant dans un modeste vase en verre.*
PAGE DE DROITE: *Dans le pavillon, la nappe matelassée sur la table rustique a été confectionnée en Inde sur des indications d'Ischa. C'est encore elle qui a choisi le ton jaune orange des murs et qui a fabriqué des rideaux avec un tissu à petits carreaux qu'elle vend dans sa boutique.*

Ansicht der Zugbrücke, die zu den »Zaanse Huisjes« führt, einem Viertel aus Holz- und Steinhäusern des 18. und 19. Jahrhunderts.

A view of the swing bridge leading to the "Zaanse Huisjes", a district where the houses are built of stone and wood and date from the 18th and 19th centuries.

Une vue sur le pont-levis qui mène aux «Zaanse Huisjes», un quartier composé de maisons en pierre et en bois datant du 18ᵉ et du 19ᵉ siècle.

NEDERLANDS OPENLUCHTMUSEUM

Gelderland

Gegen Ende des 19. Jahrhunderts gründete Artur Hazelius in Stockholm das erste Freilichtmuseum der Welt. Das Skansen-Museum war so erfolgreich, dass bald andere Länder dem schwedischen Beispiel folgten. Alte, vom Verschwinden bedrohte Gebäudetypen, ausgewählte Höfe, Privathäuser, Landhäuser, Scheunen und Handwerksbetriebe zu versetzen und neu zu arrangieren, erforderte erhebliche Anstrengungen, profunde Fachkenntnisse und einen grenzenlosen Enthusiasmus. 1912 gegründet und 1918 in Arnhem eröffnet, gehört das »Nederlands Openluchtmuseum« zu den gelungensten Exemplaren seiner Art. Schon im Eingangsbereich hat der Besucher den Eindruck, wie durch eine Zeitmaschine à la H. G. Wells das 21. Jahrhundert zu verlassen. Auf dem weitläufigen Museumsgelände kann man mit staunenden Augen die Vergangenheit entdecken: Man spaziert über schmale, von bunten Häusern gesäumte Pflastersteinstraßen oder folgt der Straße in Richtung Zugbrücke, um in der alten Bäckerei leckere Rosinenkuchen zu essen oder in einem reetgedeckten Bauernhaus, das einst am anderen Ende Hollands stand, »poffertjes« und Crêpes zu probieren. Der Zauber dieses einzigartigen Ortes lässt einen »die andere Welt« hinter dem Tor vergessen und man scheut vor dem Moment zurück, an dem man sich wieder der Realität stellen muss.

LINKS: *Ein Winkel des traditionell gestalteten Gartens ist mit Kohl bepflanzt.*
OBEN: *Ein kleiner Garten umgibt dieses Holzhaus in dem Zaandamer Viertel.*

LEFT: *cabbages in a corner of a traditional kitchen garden.*
ABOVE: *a wooden house in the Zaandam district.*

A GAUCHE: *un bout de jardin traditionnel planté de choux.*
CI-DESSUS: *Cette maison en bois du quartier zaandamois est agrémentée d'un petit jardin.*

Towards the end of the 19th century, Artur Hazelius founded the world's first open air museum in Stockholm. The Skansen Museum proved so successful that other countries lost no time in following the Swedish example. The gradual assembling of old buildings that were passing out of existence, and the putting together a selection of farms, private houses, cottages, barns and workshops, required considerable effort, knowledge and enthusiasm. Founded in 1912 in Arnhem and completed in 1918, the "Nederlands Openluchtmuseum" can boast that it is one of the most successful enterprises of its type in Europe. From the moment you enter you have the impression that you have left the 21st century behind and stepped into a Wellsian time warp. You can wander along small cobbled streets past brightly painted houses with wooden tympana decorated with garlands and volutes. You can take the path leading down to the drawbridge, there to consume a couple of plum cakes in the old bakery, or stuff yourself with "poffertjes" and pancakes in a thatched farmhouse. Transported by the magic of this unique place, you forget the other world outside the gates and put off for as long as possible your return to reality.

Vers la fin du 19ᵉ siècle, Artur Hazelius fonda à Stockholm le premier musée en plein air du monde, et le musée de Skansen connut un tel succès que, par la suite, d'autres pays se mirent à suivre l'exemple de la Suède. Cueillir ici et là des bâtiments anciens en voie de disparition et composer un échantillonnage de fermes, de demeures privées, de maisons rustiques, de granges et d'ateliers d'artisans, demande un effort considérable, des connaissances approfondies et un enthousiasme sans bornes. Fondé en 1912 et complété en 1918 à Arnhem, le «Nederlands Openluchtmuseum» peut se glorifier d'être un des exemples des plus réussis dans son genre. Le visiteur a l'impression de quitter le 21ᵉ siècle et d'entrer dans une machine à remonter le temps digne de H.G. Wells. Dans ce vaste domaine où l'on découvre le passé avec des yeux émerveillés, on peut flâner dans des petites rues pavées, bordées de maisons aux vives couleurs, coiffées d'un tympan en bois orné de guirlandes et de volutes. On peut emprunter le chemin qui mène au pont-levis pour aller s'offrir quelques bons gâteaux aux raisins dans la vieille boulangerie et on peut savourer des «poffertjes» et des crêpes dans une ferme à toit de chaume. Emportés par la magie de ce lieu unique en son genre, on oublie « l'autre monde» au-delà de la grille, et on hésite à terminer la visite et retrouver la réalité.

OBEN: *Die Dekoration in diesem Haus, das einem Kaufmann gehörte und früher in Zaanstad stand, zeugt vom Wohlstand des Bürgertums zu Anfang des 19. Jahrhunderts.*

RECHTS UND RECHTE SEITE: *Das Wohnzimmer und die Küche, die einst den Angestellten vorbehalten war, beweisen mit ihren gelb lackierten Wänden, dem Kamin mit Delfter Kacheln und dem gusseisernen Ofen, dass das Personal in den wohlhabenden Häusern behagliche Räume bewohnte.*

ABOVE: *In this merchant's house, which was moved from Zaanstad, the décor reflects the prosperity of the bourgeoisie in the early 19th-century.*

RIGHT AND FACING PAGE: *In the kitchen and living room formerly reserved for servants, the yellow-painted panels, fireplace tiled in Delft, opaline hanging lamp and cast-iron projecting stove show that the staffs of the more affluent houses were lodged very comfortably indeed.*

CI-DESSUS: *La décoration de cette maison de négociant qui se trouvait jadis à Zaanstad reflète la prospérité de la bourgeoisie vers le début du 19e siècle.*

A DROITE ET PAGE DE DROITE: *Dans le séjour et la cuisine réservée aux employés de maison, les lambris laqués jaune, le corps de cheminée carrelé en Delft, la suspension en opaline et le poêle en fonte nous prouvent que – du moins dans les grandes maisons – les pièces de service étaient agréables et confortables.*

LINKS: *Eine perfekte Darstellung der alltäglichen Glücksmomente: Pieter de Hooch, Eine Frau mit Kind und Hund stillt einen Säugling (um 1658–1660).*
RECHTE SEITE: *In der Küche einer Wäscherei, die von Overveen hierher gebracht wurde, sind die Wände vollständig mit »witjes« gekachelt.*

LEFT: *The very image of domestic bliss: Pieter de Hooch, A Woman Nursing an Infant with a Child and a Dog (c. 1658–1660).*
FACING PAGE: *In the kitchen of a laundry originating in Overveen, the walls are entirely covered in "witjes".*

A GAUCHE: *L'incarnation du bonheur quotidien: Pieter de Hooch, Femme allaitant un nouveau-né avec un chien et un chat (vers 1658–1660).*
PAGE DE DROITE: *Dans la cuisine d'une blanchisserie qui fut transportée d'Overveen, les murs sont entièrement habillés de «witjes».*

LINKE SEITE: *In einer Ecke dieses Schlafzimmers mit Holzwänden in Altrosa, steht ein Stuhl mit strohbespannter Sitzfläche unter einem kolorierten romantischen Stich.*
RECHTS: *Neben dem Alkoven findet man ein Möbel, das früher zum Falten der Wäsche benutzt wurde, damit sie sich perfekt in den großen Wäscheschränken stapeln ließ.*

FACING PAGE: *In a corner of this bedroom, with panels painted a faded pink, a straw-bottomed chair stands beneath a sentimental coloured engraving.*
RIGHT: *Beside the alcove bed is a piece of furniture which was used for folding sheets in such a way that they could be neatly stacked in the linen cupboard.*

PAGE DE GAUCHE: *Dans un coin de cette chambre à coucher dont les lambris sont laqués en vieux rose, on a posé une chaise paillée sous une gravure coloriée au sujet sentimental.*
A DROITE: *Le meuble-pressoir, à côté du lit-alcôve, servait jadis à plier le linge de telle façon qu'on pouvait ensuite le ranger impeccablement dans les grandes armoires.*

KASTEEL MIDDACHTEN
Isabelle en Aurel, gravin en graaf Ortenburg-Bentinck
Gelderland

Das stolze »Kasteel Middachten« hat etwas Magisches und es ist schwer zu sagen, ob das an der strengen und eleganten Architektur liegt oder an dem Umstand, dass es sich einsam, umgeben von einem Garten im französischen Stil, aus einer großen Wasserfläche erhebt. Zwischen 1694 und 1697 vom Herrn von Middachten, Godard van Reede, auf den Überresten einer mittelalterlichen Burg erbaut, die von französischen Truppen zerstört worden war, entstand Middachten in seiner heutigen Form nach den Plänen der Architekten Jacob Roman und Steven Vennekool. Doch der besondere Charme dieses ungewöhnlichen Schlosses ist nur teilweise auf seine beeindruckende Architektur und das monumentale Treppenhaus zurückzuführen. Im Gegensatz zu anderen Bauten aus der gleichen Epoche und mit der gleichen Bedeutung besitzt Middachten eine überraschende Intimität. Nichts stört die heitere Atmosphäre in der original erhaltenen Küche, dem Esszimmer, den geräumigen eleganten Salons oder den Schlafzimmern mit reich drapierten Himmelbetten. Heute setzen sich die Eigentümer des Schlosses, der Graf und die Gräfin Ortenburg-Bentinck, dafür ein, das einzigartige Ambiente zu bewahren. Ihnen verdanken wir, dass Middachten die Besucher weiterhin verzaubert.

Detail eines weißen Marmorwaschbeckens mit Masken-Ornament vom Ende des 17. Jahrhunderts.

Detail of a late 17th-century white marble washbasin with its "mascherone".

Gros plan sur une fontaine murale en marbre blanc, fin 17ᵉ, ornée d'un mascaron.

There is something magical about the proud castle of Middachten, and it's hard to say whether this derives from the austere and elegant architecture of the place or from its solitary site in the middle of a great expanse of water, which is itself encircled by a park of French design. First built between 1694 and 1697 by the Lord of Middachten, Godard van Reede, on the ruins of a mediaeval fortress sacked and destroyed by French troops, Middachten was rebuilt in its present form by the architects Jacob Roman and Steven Vennekool. But it is neither the imposing architecture of the building, nor its monumental staircase, that gives Middachten its unique charm. The fact is that unlike other buildings of the same period and similar importance, Middachten has a surprising level of intimacy. From the totally unaltered kitchen to the dining room, the broad, elegant salons, and the bedrooms upstairs with their richly draped four-posters, nothing disturbs the steady atmosphere of warmth and welcome exuded by this house. The owners of the castle, Count and Countess Ortenburg-Bentinck, have waged a long campaign to preserve the ambience of their home. And it is thanks to their efforts that the magic of Middachten continues to enchant all who go there.

Das Wirtschaftshaus von der Brücke aus gesehen, die das »Oostelijk Bouwhuis«, das ehemalige Lagerhaus, mit der Orangerie verbindet.

The estate offices seen from the bridge that links the "Oostelijk Bouwhuis", an old warehouse, with the orangery garden.

Les communs vus du pont qui relie le «Oostelijk Bouwhuis», un ancien entrepôt, à l'orangerie.

Il a quelque chose de magique, le fier château de Middachten, et on ignore si cela tient à son architecture à la fois sévère et élégante ou au fait qu'il se dresse, solitaire, au milieu d'une vaste pièce d'eau entourée d'un parc à la française. Construit entre 1694 et 1697 par Godard van Reede, seigneur de Middachten, sur les vestiges d'un château fort médiéval saccagé par les troupes françaises, Middachten prit la forme qu'on lui connaît aujourd'hui grâce aux architectes Jacob Roman et Steven Vennekool. Mais ni l'architecture imposante du château, ni sa cage d'escalier monumentale ne constituent le charme particulier de cette demeure exceptionnelle. Middachten, contrairement à d'autres bâtiments de la même époque et de la même envergure, possède un caractère intime qui ne cesse de surprendre. De la cuisine intacte à la salle à manger, et des vastes salons élégants aux chambres à coucher meublées de lits à baldaquins richement drapés, rien ne vient troubler la sérénité des lieux. De nos jours, les propriétaires du château, le comte et la comtesse Ortenburg-Bentinck, se battent pour préserver cette ambiance sans pareille. Grâce à eux, la magie de Middachten continue d'enchanter ses visiteurs.

Die majestätische Kuppel des Architekten Jacob Roman ist mit Stuck- und Holzelementen von Steven Vennekool geschmückt.

The majestic dome built by the architect Jacob Roman was decorated with wood and stucco elements sculpted by Steven Vennekool.

La coupole majestueuse due à l'architecte Jacob Roman a été décorée avec des éléments en stuc et en bois sculpté par Steven Vennekool.

OBEN: *In einem der geräumigen Schlafzimmer teilt sich das große Himmelbett den Platz mit einem Canapé und einem Sesselpaar mit Überzügen in bester viktorianischer Tradition.*

RECHTS: *In Middachten findet man immer prächtige Blumensträuße, gekonnt arrangiert vom treuen Andries.*

RECHTE SEITE: *In einem der Salons im Erdgeschoss verweilt ein Sonnenstrahl auf einem Sessel im Louis-Quinze-Stil.*

ABOVE: *in one of the spacious bedrooms on the first floor, a large four-poster bed and a couple of upholstered chairs in the best Victorian tradition.*

RIGHT: *Middachten is full of stunning flower arrangements skilfully put together by Andries.*

FACING PAGE: *In one of the downstairs rooms a ray of sunlight lingers on a solitary Louis-Quinze armchair.*

CI-DESSUS: *Dans une des vastes chambres à coucher du premier étage, un grand lit à dais se partage l'espace avec un canapé et une paire de chaises houssées dans la meilleure tradition victorienne.*

A DROITE: *A Middachten il y a toujours de somptueux bouquets, arrangés de main de maître par le fidèle Andries.*

PAGE DE DROITE: *Dans un des salons du rez-de-chaussée, un rayon de soleil s'attarde sur un fauteuil doré de style Louis Quinze.*

LINKS: *Im »Onderhuis« sind die Küchen, die Dienstbotenzimmer und die Waschküche untergebracht. Stilecht ist die strohgelbe Farbe der Möbel und der Vitrinenschränke.*
RECHTE SEITE: *Die große Anzahl von »modernen« Küchengeräten auf dem soliden Arbeitstisch und auf dem Sims der Fensternische zeugt von emsiger Betriebsamkeit.*

LEFT: *The "Onderhuis" comprises the kitchens, staff quarters and laundry room. The butter-yellow colour of the furniture and the glass-fronted cabinets is traditional in this part of Holland.*
FACING PAGE: *The "modern" kitchen utensils on the table and in the window embrasure attest to a steady level of activity in the cooking department.*

A GAUCHE: *Le «Onderhuis» loge les cuisines, les quartiers du personnel et la buanderie. Traditionnelle, la couleur «beurre frais» des meubles et des armoires vitrées.*
PAGE DE DROITE: *Sur la solide table de travail et dans l'embrasure de la fenêtre, la présence d'un grand nombre d'ustensiles de cuisine «modernes» témoigne d'une activité fiévreuse.*

RECHTS: *Das alte Grammophon in der Wäscherei belegt, dass bei den Wasch- und Bügelfrauen Entspannung nicht zu kurz kam.*

RIGHT: *An old-fashioned gramophone in the laundry room accompanied the ladies who did the washing and ironing as they worked.*

A DROITE: *Dans la buanderie, la présence d'un vieux gramophone prouve que les repasseuses et les lingères pensaient aussi aux douces heures de détente.*

De Heeren van Bronkhorst

Gelderland

Das Städtchen Bronkhorst im Osten der Niederlande hat etwas so Unwirkliches, dass man sich wie der belgische Schriftsteller Georges Rodenbach unweigerlich fragt, »ob nicht ein Museum daraus würde, wenn man eine Glaskuppel darüber bauen würde« … Frans Koekkoek und Evert Warffemius kommt es so vor, als habe das schlichte Haus mit der Scheune und dem weitläufigen angrenzenden Gelände nur auf sie gewartet. Es erschien ihnen geradezu dafür geschaffen, hier ihr Antiquitätengeschäft und Zuhause einzurichten. Dennoch hätten sie nie damit gerechnet, so eine seltene Perle in einem Naturschutzgebiet zu finden – in einem Ort, der nur aus einigen Straßen, Gassen und einer kleinen Kirche besteht, und wo jedes Haus, jeder Fensterladen, jeder Ziegelstein, jede Fliese und jeder Pflasterstein liebevoll instand gehalten wird. Frans und Evert mögen die leise Stimmung des Ortes, in dem fast nichts an das 21. Jahrhundert erinnert. Ihren Rückzug in die Vergangenheit betonend, haben sie sich ein Ambiente geschaffen, in dem der mit Delfter Kacheln verzierte Kamin, der mit blau-weißen Fayencen gefüllte Vitrinenschrank aus Nussbaum und die alte Küche, die herrlich nach Zimt und Apfelkuchen duftet, uns von der friedlichen Zeit erzählen, in der die Menschen ihr Leben noch nach dem Rhythmus der großen Kirchenuhr ausrichteten.

LINKS: *Besucher läuten die Glocke.*
OBEN: *Der Steingutteller mit der Inschrift sagt mehr als tausend Höflichkeiten.*
VORHERGEHENDE DOPPELSEITE: *Bronkhorst und Umgebung.*

LEFT: *Visitors ring a bell.*
ABOVE: *A plate sets the essential tone.*
PREVIOUS PAGES: *Bronkhorst and its environs.*

A GAUCHE: *Le sou de la clochette annonce l'arrivée des visiteurs.*
CI-DESSUS: *Une assiette en faïence où l'on peut lire «Bienvenue – entrez» en dit plus que mille politesses.*
DOUBLE PAGE PRÉCÉDENTE: *Bronkhorst et ses environs.*

The little town of Bronkhorst in the east of Holland has something unreal about it, so much so that one actually wonders whether it wouldn't instantly turn into a museum exhibit if you put it under glass. Frans Koekkoek and Evert Warffemius are convinced that their modest house with its barn and surrounding land was actively awaiting them – that they were somehow predestined to make the place their home and incidentally their antique shop. Be that as it may, it was no easy task to unearth a pearl this rare in a protected site composed of a few streets and alleys clustered round a tiny church. In Bronkhorst, every house, every shutter, every brick, tile and cobblestone has been lovingly preserved. Frans and Evert love the noiseless atmosphere of Bronkhorst, where practically nothing is present to remind them of the 21st-century. To emphasize their detachment even further, they have created an interior in which the fireplace is decorated with Delft tiles, the walnut dresser is filled with blue and white earthenware, and the old kitchen is perfumed by the scent of cinnamon and apples from tarts baking in the oven. All these things speak to us of a more peaceful time, in which our lives, like those of the people of Bronkhorst, were regulated by the chimes of a church clock.

Vor dem Haus bietet eine Bank mit der Inschrift »De Heeren van Bronkhorst« müden Spaziergängern eine Rastmöglichkeit.

A bench in front of the house bearing the legend "De Heeren van Bronkhorst" invites the weary passer-by to stop and rest.

Devant la maison, un banc orné de l'inscription «De Heeren van Bronkhorst» invite les promeneurs fatigués à se reposer.

La petite ville de Bronkhorst, à l'est des Pays-Bas, a quelque chose d'irréel et, avec l'écrivain belge Georges Rodenbach, on se demande si Bronkhorst ne deviendrait pas un musée si on mettait un couvercle sur la ville. Frans Koekkoek et Evert Warffemius sont persuadés que la modeste maison avec sa grange et son vaste terrain attenant les attendait et qu'ils étaient prédestinés à y installer leur magasin d'antiquités et leur demeure privée. Quoi qu'il en soit, il ne semble pas évident d'avoir trouvé cette perle rare dans un site protégé constitué de quelques rares rues et ruelles et d'une petite église. Ici chaque maison, chaque volet, chaque brique, chaque carreau et chaque pavé a été préservé avec amour. Frans et Evert adorent cette ambiance feutrée où rien, ou presque, n'évoque le 21e siècle. D'ailleurs, pour bien souligner leur détachement, ils se sont créé un intérieur où la cheminée décorée de carreaux de Delft, le vaisselier en noyer rempli de faïences bleues et blanches et la vieille cuisine qui sent bon la cannelle et le gâteau aux pommes tout chaud, nous parlent d'un temps paisible où les habitants de Bronkhorst vivaient encore au rythme des heures indiquées par la grande horloge de l'église.

In einem hautfarben gestrichenen Aufsatzschrank zeigen Evert und Frans einen Teil ihrer chinesischen Porzellansammlung aus dem 18. Jahrhundert.

Part of Evert and Frans's collection of 18th-century Chinese porcelain, on a dresser painted blush pink.

Dans une armoire vitrée dont l'intérieur a été peint en «cuisse de nymphe émue», Evert et Frans exposent une partie de leur collection de porcelaines de Chine 18e.

LINKS: *Ein chinesischer Porzellanhund und ein winziger Rahmen mit dem Porträt einer Dame aus der Empirezeit wurden wegen ihrer frischen Farben kombiniert.*
LINKE SEITE: *In der gemütlichen Küche bilden die Pendeluhr, der Samowar und das Hundebild aus Delfter Kacheln typische Bestandteile eines holländischen Interieurs.*

LEFT: *A Chinese porcelain dog and an Empire medallion-portrait of a lady of quality have been placed here on account of their fresh colours.*
FACING PAGE: *A clock, a samovar and a Delft picture of a seated dog are the main elements in the kitchen's typically Dutch interior.*

A GAUCHE: *Un chien en porcelaine de Chine et un médaillon représentant une dame de qualité d'époque Empire ont été choisis pour la fraîcheur de leurs coloris.*
PAGE DE GAUCHE: *Dans la cuisine intime, la pendule, le samovar et le tableau en Delft représentant un chien assis forment les éléments principaux d'un intérieur typiquement hollandais.*

RECHTS: *Eine der Hündinnen – Farah – hat einen behaglichen Platz vor dem Feuer gefunden. Bald wird mit dem Wasser in dem großen Kupferkessel ein köstlicher chinesischer Tee zubereitet.*
FOLGENDE DOPPELSEITE: *Sich wohlfühlen wird bei Frans und Evert großgeschrieben: Mit Begeisterung entziffern sie alte Bücher oder ziehen sich auf ein weiches Bett-Sofa mit einem Überwurf mit Wappendekor zurück. Die Hündin Ena genießt Letzteres ebenfalls.*

RIGHT: *Farah, a real dog, relaxing in front of the wood fire. The copper kettle is often in service for making China tea.*

FOLLOWING PAGES: *A sense of well-being pervades Frans and Evert's home. One might peruse a precious book or follow the example of their dog Ena, and snuggle up on the soft velvet sofa decorated with coats of arms.*

A DROITE: *Une des chiennes au joli nom de Farah a trouvé une place très agréable devant le feu de bois. Tout à l'heure la grosse bouilloire en cuivre servira à préparer un délicat thé de Chine.*
DOUBLE PAGE SUIVANTE: *Chez Frans et Evert, tout est prétexte au bien-être: déchiffrer avec fascination un livre ancien ou se retirer sur le canapé-lit moelleux recouvert d'un tissu décoré d'armoiries. La chienne Ena est tout à fait de leur avis.*

KASTEEL TWICKEL
Gravin en graaf zu Castell Rudenhausen
Overijssel

Nur wenige holländische Schlösser können sich einer ähnlich reichen Vergangenheit rühmen wie »Kasteel Twickel«. Die Dynastien verschiedener großer Adelshäuser, wie etwa die Familie van Wassenaer Obdam oder die Aldenburg Bentincks, haben jede für sich der soliden, strengen Architektur ihre eigene Prägung gegeben. Das im westfälischen Stil gehaltene Wasserschloss, dessen Ursprünge bis ins 14. Jahrhundert zurückreichen und dessen Eingangsbereich von einem Skulpturenpaar, Adam und Eva, geschmückt wird, erlebte zahlreiche eindrucksvolle Metamorphosen. So wurde beispielsweise das im Jahr 1692 errichtete Treppenhaus von Jacob Roman entworfen, dem Architekten des Königspalastes »Het Loo« bei Apeldoorn. An dieser Stelle sollte auch erwähnt werden, dass der englische König Georg I. auf der Durchreise in Twickel im Jahr 1727 angeblich so viele Melonen verspeiste, dass er anschließend in Osnabrück starb. Doch das eigentlich Faszinierende sind die Interieurs, die aus Marmor, norwegischem Basalt, Stuck und Cordoba-Leder gestaltet wurden. Und auch die Eichenvertäfelungen, das Porzellan aus China und Japan, die Möbel, die Gemälde und die Bibliothek mit seltenen Ausgaben erzählen vom Leben der Herren und Edelfräulein, deren Spuren sich hier noch immer finden.

LINKS: *Eine Steintreppe und eine breite Brücke führen zum beeindruckenden Eingang des »Kasteel Twickel«.*
OBEN: *eine mit einem Löwenkopf verzierte Bleiurne aus dem 19. Jahrhundert.*

LEFT: *A stone staircase and a broad bridge lead to the imposing entrance of "Kasteel Twickel".*
ABOVE: *a 19th-century lead urn with a lion's head.*

A GAUCHE: *Un escalier de pierre et un large pont mènent à l'entrée imposante de «Kasteel Twickel».*
CI-DESSUS: *Une urne 19ᵉ en plomb est ornée d'une tête de lion.*

Few buildings in Holland can boast a past or even an architectural history as rich as Twickel Castle. The successive reigns there of great noble families such as the van Wassenaer Obdams and the Aldenburg Bentincks have all left their mark on this solid, rather severe construction with its entrance adorned by statues of Adam and Eve. Twickel is a "Wasserschloss" of the Westphalian type with parts dating back to the 14th century, and over the years it has witnessed a number of spectacular changes. The staircase, built in 1692, was designed by Jacob Roman who was the architect of the "Het Loo" Palace near Apeldoorn. George I of England died at Osnabrück in 1727 as a consequence of eating too many melons while staying at Twickel. And so forth. As far as we are concerned, Twickel's chief merit resides in its magnificent interiors, which include fine work in marble and Norwegian basalt, splendid stuccoes, and the rarest Cordoba leather and oak panelling. There are also superb collections of Chinese and Japanese porcelain, furniture, paintings, and rare books. All these things recall the times when Twickel was the abode of great lords and ladies, whose shades still haunt many a room.

Die große Statue von Adam an der Fassade scheint aufmerksam das Gewächshaus zu beobachten.

A burly statue of Adam against the façade contemplates the plain architecture of the orangery.

Adossée à la façade, la grande statue d'Adam semble observer attentivement la sobre construction de l'orangerie.

Très peu de châteaux en Hollande peuvent s'enorgueillir d'un passé historique et architectural aussi riche que le château de Twickel. Les dynasties successives des grandes familles nobles telles que les van Wassenaer Obdam et les Aldenburg Bentinck ont marqué de leur empreinte cette solide construction sévère dont l'entrée est agrémentée d'une paire de statues représentant Adam et Eve. Le château de type westphalien entouré d'eau et dont les origines remontent au 14ᵉ siècle fut le sujet d'une série de métamorphoses impressionnantes. La cage d'escalier, construite en 1692, porte la signature de Jacob Roman, l'architecte du Palais Royal «Het Loo» tout près d'Apeldoorn. Mentionnons au passage que le roi d'Angleterre, George Iᵉʳ, de passage à Twickel en 1727, y mangea un si grand nombre de melons qu'il mourut par la suite à Osnabrück! Disons avant tout que Twickel renferme une série d'intérieurs fascinants où domine le marbre, le basalte norvégien, les stucs, le cuir de Cordoue, les lambris en chêne, les porcelaines de Chine et du Japon; ici les meubles, les tableaux et la bibliothèque aux volumes rares font revivre l'époque des Grands Seigneurs et des Belles Dames dont le souvenir hante encore les salons.

In einem der Schlafzimmer ruht eine Hand aus Bronze auf einem prächtigen Kissen.

A bronze hand resting on a rich cushion in one of the bedrooms.

Une main en bronze repose sur un coussin somptueux dans une des chambres à coucher.

LINKS: *Die viktoriani-
schen Sessel neben dem
prächtigen barocken
Kamin laden zum
Entspannen ein.*
RECHTE SEITE: *Die
»Drostenkamer«, (Rich-
terzimmer) wurde im
Neo-Rokoko-Stil deko-
riert. Der Kamin des
Antwerpener Bildhauers
und Architekten Jan
Pieter van Baurscheit
wurde 1897 eingebaut.*

LEFT: *an inviting
armchair in Victorian
style beside the magni-
ficent fireplace.*
FACING PAGE: *In
the "Drostenkamer"
(Judges' Chamber) dec-
orated in neo-rococo,
there is a spectacular
fireplace by the Antwerp
sculptor and architect
Jan Pieter van Baur-
scheit. The piece was
added to the décor in
1897.*

A GAUCHE: *Il fait bon
se reposer dans un des
fauteuils victoriens près
de la cheminée baroque.*
PAGE DE DROITE:
*Dans la «Drosten-
kamer» (Chambre des
juges) – décorée dans
un style néo-rococo, une
cheminée spectaculaire,
œuvre de l'architecte et
sculpteur anversois Jan
Pieter van Baurscheit, a
été intégrée en 1897.*

LINKS: *Die ganze Ele-
ganz des französischen
18. Jahrhunderts zeigt
sich an dieser Louis-
Seize-Uhr aus Marmor
und vergoldeter Bronze.*
RECHTS: *Auf einem
Louis-Quinze-Sekretär
leistet ein vergoldeter
Kerzenständer aus
Bronze der Schokola-
dentasse mit Deckel
Gesellschaft.*

LEFT: *All the elegance
of the French 18th cen-
tury is concentrated in
this Louis-Seize marble
and gilt-bronze clock.*
RIGHT: *Standing on
the Louis-Quinze desk
are a gilt-bronze*

*candlestick and an
ornate chocolate cup
complete with lid.*

A GAUCHE: *On re-
trouve toute l'élégance
du style français 18ᵉ
dans cette pendule
d'époque Louis Seize en
marbre et en bronze
doré.*
A DROITE: *Sur un
secrétaire à abattant
Louis Quinze, une tasse
à chocolat munie d'un
couvercle tient compag-
nie à un bougeoir en
bronze doré.*

LINKE SEITE: *In der Küche vom Anfang des 20. Jahrhunderts faszinieren besonders die Spüle aus massivem Holz und die Kupfertöpfe und -pfannen, die früher von den Angestellten ungefähr sechsmal im Jahr poliert wurden.*
RECHTS: *Die Mauer im Treppenhaus nahe der Dienstbotenkammer ist mit einem hübschen Wandbild aus Delfter Porzellan dekoriert.*

FACING PAGE: *The most striking features in the early 20th-century kitchen are a solid wood sink and a copper "batterie de cuisine" — which is polished, on average, six times a year.*
RIGHT: *The wall of the landing by the butler's pantry is decorated with a beautiful Delft plaque.*

PAGE DE GAUCHE: *Dans la cuisine, qui date du début du 20e siècle, on remarque surtout l'évier en bois massif et la batterie de cuisine en cuivre que les domestiques polissent en moyenne six fois par an.*
A DROITE: *Le mur du palier près du «butler's pantry» est orné d'une jolie plaque en Delft.*

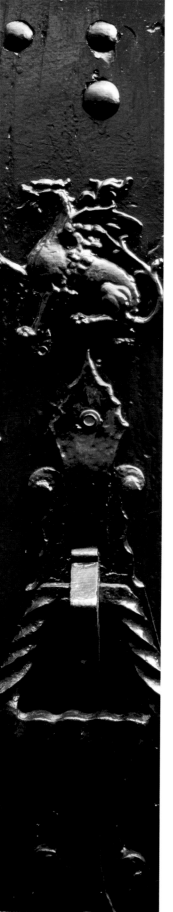

HISTORISCH WOONMUSEUM DON QUICHOTTE

Frits Fritsen

Noord-Brabant

Immer schon träumte der Gebäudemaler Frits Fritsen davon, ein edler Ritter zu sein und wie Lancelot in einer Burg mit Zugbrücke und Bergfried zu wohnen. Da Frits Fritsen aber einsehen musste, dass die Ära der Tafelrunde längst vorüber ist, beschloss er, seinen Traum in dem Garten hinter seinem kleinen Vorstadthaus bei 's-Hertogenbosch zu realisieren. Manche halten Fritsen für einen Visionär der wie Ferdinand Cheval ein Meisterwerk der fantastischen Architektur geschaffen hat. Andere wiederum belächeln den »armen Ritter Frits«, der tatsächlich seinen schönen Blumengarten zerstört und Berge von Erde und Steinen bewegt hat, um die Kitschburg »Don Quichotte« zu erbauen. Genau wie die tragischen Helden von Cervantes hat der mutige Fritsen gegen alle Spötter und die Windmühlenflügel der Bürokratie gekämpft, die sich gegen seine Ritterarchitektur gestellt hatten. Aber er hat letztlich die Schlacht gewonnen und fühlt sich in seinem mehr oder weniger zeitgetreuen Kostüm offensichtlich pudelwohl. In seinem Mini-Camelot stellt er heute seine Sammlung alter Rüstungen und Waffen aus und hier zieht er das Schwert, um seinen Kritikern zu zeigen, wer der Herr von »Don Quichotte« ist.

LINKS: *Das eiserne Eingangstor ziert ein Fabelwesen aus dem Mittelalter.*
OBEN: *Detail vom Kopfende des reich verzierten Betts.*

LEFT: *The ironwork of the front door is crowned by a mediaeval mythical creature.*
ABOVE: *detail of the Fritsens' richly decorated, ceremonial bedhead.*

A GAUCHE: *La ferronnerie de la porte d'entrée est couronnée d'un animal mythique moyenâgeux.*
CI-DESSUS: *détail de la tête de lit richement décorée du lit d'apparat.*

Frits Fritsen, a housepainter living in a small cottage near 's-Hertogenbosch, had always daydreamed of being a noble knight like Sir Lancelot, in a fortress with a drawbridge and a great frowning keep. But knowing very well that an Arthurian castle was far beyond his means, he decided to make his dream a reality at the bottom of his suburban garden. Some claim that Mr. Fritsen is a visionary like Ferdinand Cheval, who created what has turned out to be one of the masterpieces of "art fantastique". Others make fun of "poor Sir Frits", who was brave enough to destroy his pretty flower garden and move mountains of earth and stone in order to build a monument of kitsch which he dubbed "Don Quixote". Like Cervantes' tragic hero, Frits Fritsen had to strive mightily against the mockers, tilting again and again at the windmills of bureaucracy that thwarted him at every turn. In the end he triumphed and may yet be found in his mini-Camelot, attired in more or less period costume, fiercely brandishing a sword and displaying his collection of quite authentic arms and armour to anyone who cares to visit.

Il fut un temps où le peintre en bâtiment Frits Fritsen rêvait d'être un noble chevalier de l'envergure d'un Lancelot et d'habiter un château fort avec un pont-levis et un donjon majestueux. Réalisant toutefois que l'époque des chevaliers de la Table Ronde était bien lointaine, il décida de concrétiser son rêve au fond du jardinet de sa modeste maison près de 's-Hertogenbosch. Certains prétendent que Fritsen est un représentant de l'architecture fantastique comme le célèbre facteur cheval, mais d'autres se moquent ouvertement de ce «pauvre Chevalier Frits» qui eut le courage de détruire son joli jardin fleuri et de déplacer des montagnes de terre et des tonnes de pierres pour bâtir un ensemble kitsch baptisé «Don Quichotte». Comme le héros tragique de Cervantès, le courageux Fritsen a défié les railleurs et s'est battu contre les moulins à vents de la bureaucratie qui s'opposait à cette architecture chevaleresque. Mais finalement, il a gagné son pari et en profite pour s'habiller en costume – vaguement – d'époque. Fritsen se sent parfaitement heureux dans son mini-Camelot. C'est ici qu'il expose sa collection d'armures et d'armes anciennes authentiques et qu'il brandit son épée pour prouver à ses adversaires qu'à «Don Quichotte», il est encore et toujours le maître des lieux.

LINKS: *Im Eingangs-bereich stellt der Haus-herr einen Teil seiner Sammlung alter Rüstungen aus.*

RECHTE SEITE: *Auch wenn die Gegenstände nicht immer authentisch sind, so verfügt Frits doch über das Talent, eine romantische Atmosphäre zu erzeugen.*

LEFT: *Part of Frits Fritsen's collection of arms and armour is displayed in his front hall.*

FACING PAGE: *Frits has a knack for creating an atmosphere of true romance, even though much of his décor isn't necessarily "d'époque".*

A GAUCHE: *Dans l'entrée, le maître des lieux a exposé une partie de sa collection d'armures anciennes.*

PAGE DE DROITE: *Frits a le don de créer une ambiance romantique, même si les éléments de la décoration ne sont pas toujours d'époque.*

RECHTS: *In Sachen Inneneinrichtung ist Fritsen sicherlich kein Purist, was erklärt, wieso er zu einem alten Kohleofen zwei flämische Neo-Renaissance-Stühle aus dem 19. Jahrhundert stellt.*

RIGHT: *Frits is no purist and doesn't claim to be one – hence the cast-iron charcoal stove set between a couple of 19th-century neo-Renaissance Flemish chairs.*

A DROITE: *En tant que décorateur, Fritsen n'est pas un puriste, ce qui explique pourquoi un poêle de «grand-mère» est flanqué d'une paire de chaises 19ᵉ de style néo-Renaissance flamand.*

LINKS: *Apotheose des Kitsch oder do-it-yourself-Meisterwerk? Eine Fülle von »barocken« Dekorationselementen ziert das Prunkbett, ein Meisterstück von Fritsen.*

RECHTE SEITE: *Zu einem Schloss gehören auch religiöse Kunstwerke. Frits konnte diesem aus Gips gefertigten Christus am Kreuz nicht widerstehen. Das Gewand gehört seiner Frau.*

LEFT: *Ultimate kitsch or masterpiece of do-it-yourself? The ceremonial bed – made by Frits Fritsen – is drenched in baroque ornament.*

FACING PAGE: *Any chateau worth its salt contains a few pieces of religious art, and "Don Quichotte" is no exception. The chatelaine's costume belongs to Mrs Fritsen.*

A GAUCHE: *Apothéose du kitsch ou chef-d'œuvre du bricolage? Le lit d'apparat – une pièce de maîtrise signée Fritsen – est revêtu d'innombrables décorations baroques.*

PAGE DE DROITE: *Tout château digne de ce nom renferme des œuvres d'art religieux et Frits n'a pas pu résister à une Crucifixion en plâtre. Le costume de châtelaine appartient à son épouse.*

CORNELIS LE MAIR

Noord-Brabant

In den Niederlanden nennt man ihn den »Paganini der Leinwand«
und seine Bewunderer vergleichen ihn mit den großen Meistern des
17. Jahrhunderts. Aber Cornelis Le Mair, den gute Freunde Cees
nennen, lehnt jeden Vergleich mit seinen berühmten Kollegen ab
und betont die Eigenständigkeit seiner Motive und Technik. Cees
lebt in einem alten Bauernhof bei Eindhoven und im Lauf der Jahre
hat er auch aus seinem Garten und seinem Haus ein wahres Kunst-
werk gemacht, in dem es sich zwischen den Hunden, Katzen, Hüh-
nern und Ziegen gut leben lässt. Hier »regiert« der Hausherr, lang-
haarig wie einst Molière, mit Schnurrbart und Kinnbärtchen à la
Rembrandt und einem Kleidungsstil, der irgendwo zwischen einem
Hippie und einem Marquis aus dem 18. Jahrhundert anzusiedeln ist.
Die Leinwand füllt er mit Nymphen, Darstellungen von Leda und
Diana sowie zahllosen Rosen und Landschaften wie in Gemälden
von Jacob van Ruisdael. Cees liebt es, die Betten mit indischen
Stoffen zu drapieren und die Decken mit exotischen Lampen zu
schmücken. Seine chinesischen Vasen harmonieren ohne Weiteres
mit den selbst gebauten Musikinstrumenten und das Delfter Porzellan steht in dekorativem Gegensatz zu den prächtigen Kacheln, die
er aus Isfahan mitgebracht hat. Wie sagte bereits Voltaire im »Candide«: »Alles wendet sich zum Besten in der besten aller Welten!«

LINKS: *Bei Le Mair
wird eine schlichte
Obstschale zu einem
malerischen Still-Leben.*
OBEN: *Von seinen
Fernreisen bringt Cees
oft kleine Keramiksta-
tuen wie diesen Tem-
peldrachen mit.*

LEFT: *At Le Mair's
house, an ordinary dish
of fruit is transformed
into a classic still life.*
ABOVE: *Cees has
brought home numer-
ous ceramic statuettes
from his travels in the
Far East, notably this
temple dragon.*

A GAUCHE: *Chez Le
Mair, une coupe de
fruits toute simple de-
vient une nature morte.*
CI-DESSUS: *De ses
voyages en Extrême-
Orient, Cees ramène
souvent des statuettes en
céramique tel ce dragon
de temple.*

In Holland he is known as the "Paganini of the Paintbrush" and his admirers unhesitatingly compare him with the great 17th-century masters: but the painter Cornelis Le Mair – Cees to his friends – refuses any comparison with his illustrious colleagues and insists only on the originality of his subject matter and his virtuoso technique. Cees lives in an old farmhouse near Eindhoven and over the years he has transformed his house and garden into a work of art in its own right, which he inhabits in company with dogs, cats, hens, pigeons and goats. Here he reigns supreme, long-haired like Molière with a Rembrandt-style goatee and moustache. His clothes are part hippie, part 18th-century marquis, and he paints canvases replete with nymphs, Ledas, Dianas, roses and Jacob van Ruisdael landscapes. His beds are draped with Indian embroidered fabrics and his ceilings are hung with exotic lanterns; his Chinese porcelain vases marry perfectly with the musical instruments he makes and decorates with his own hands; and his collection of Delft china supplies a delightful counterpoint to the magnificent tiles he brought home from Isphahan. Indeed everything here is for the best, in the best of all possible worlds.

Das Gewächshaus errichtete der Hobbyarchitekt Le Mair, die Urne aus Ton im Garten stammt aus dem 19. Jahrhundert.

The greenhouse was designed by architect Le Mair, but the terracotta urn dates from the 19th century.

La serre est l'œuvre de l'amateur architecte Le Mair, mais l'urne en terre cuite date du 19ᵉ siècle.

Aux Pays-Bas, on l'appelle «le Paganini du pinceau», et ses admirateurs le comparent sans hésiter aux grands maîtres du 17ᵉ siècle. Mais le peintre Cornelis Le Mair, Cees pour les intimes, refuse quant à lui toute comparaison avec ses illustres collègues et insiste sur l'originalité de ses sujets et de sa technique virtuose. Cees vit dans une vieille ferme du coté d'Eindhoven. Au cours des années, il a transformé son jardin et sa maison en une véritable œuvre d'art dans laquelle il fait bon vivre parmi les chiens, les chats, les poules, les pigeons et les chèvres. Ici, le maître des lieux arbore des cheveux longs à la Molière, moustache et barbichette rembrandtesque – sa tenue vestimentaire tient à la fois du hippie et du marquis 18ᵉ –, tout en peignant ses toiles peuplées de nymphes, de Lédas et de Dianes et d'une avalanche de roses et de paysages à la Jacob van Ruisdael. Cees adore draper ses lits de repos de tissus indiens brodés et ne peut s'empêcher de décorer ses plafonds avec des lanternes exotiques. Chez lui, les potiches chinoises se marient parfaitement aux instruments de musique qu'il a construits et décorés de ses propres mains et le Delft s'alterne allègrement avec des carreaux splendides rapportés d'Ispahan. Comme on peut lire dans le «Candide» de Voltaire: «tout va pour le mieux dans le meilleur des mondes.»

»Memento Mori« – Cees betrachtet einen menschlichen Schädel, der später auf einem »Vanitas«-Still-Leben auftauchen wird.

"Memento Mori" – Cees contemplates a human skull which will later feature in one of his "Vanitas" paintings.

«Memento mori» – Cees étudie un crâne humain qui figurera sur une de ses «vanitas».

173   NOORD-BRABANT

LINKS: *Die schillernden Farben und Stoffe bringen das Flair von Zigeunerwagen und Hippiekommunen in das Haus von Cees.*
RECHTE SEITE: *Im Schlafzimmer, das mit Schätzen aus Indien prall gefüllt ist, findet sich auch ein Modell seines Traumhauses, bei dem sich orientalische Elemente mit russischer und holländischer Volkskunst mischen.*

LEFT: *Part gipsy caravan, part hippie pad, Cees's house is full of colours and glimmering fabrics.*
FACING PAGE: *The master's bedroom is stuffed with treasures brought back from India. It also contains his model "Dream House", variously inspired by the Orient, Russian folklore, and his native Holland.*

A GAUCHE: *Mi-roulotte de romanichelle, mi-gîte de hippie, la maison de Cees regorge de couleurs et de tissus chatoyants.*
PAGE DE DROITE: *Dans la chambre de maître, bourrée de trésors venant de l'Inde, se trouve aussi la maquette de sa Maison de Rêve inspirée par l'Orient, le folklore russe et sa Hollande natale.*

OBEN: *Frans Francken d.J., Ein Sammlerkabinett (1619): Die Sammlerstube ist voll von seltenen Muscheln, wertvollen Medaillons, Manuskripten, Kunstobjekten, Zeichnungen, Blumen, Schmuck und herrlichen Gemälden.*

ABOVE: *Frans Francken the Younger, A Collector's Cabinet (1619): A collector's room, filled with rare shells, medallions, manuscripts, objets d'art, drawings, flowers, gems and magnificent paintings.*

CI-DESSUS: *Frans Francken, Un cabinet de collectionneur (1619): L'antre du collectionneur regorge de coquillages rares, de médaillons précieux, de manuscrits, d'objets d'art, de dessins, de fleurs, de bijoux et de tableaux magnifiques.*

RECHTE SEITE: *Le Mair ist auch ein begabter Porträtmaler, wie sein »Junges Mädchen mit Blumenstrauß« zeigt.*

FACING PAGE: *Le Mair also excels in portraiture. His "Young Girl with a Bunch of Flowers" proves it.*

PAGE DE DROITE: *Le Mair excelle aussi dans l'art du portrait. Sa «Jeune fille au bouquet de fleurs» en est la preuve.*

RECHTS: *Der Arbeitstisch des Künstlers wirkt wie eines seiner Still-Leben.*

FOLGENDE DOPPEL-SEITE: *Cees liebt Farben und sein Faible für Orange, Kobaltblau und Safrangelb spiegelt sich in den Stoffen, Kacheln, indischen Schals und dem Porzellan wieder, die er von seinen Fernreisen mitgebracht hat. Aus Kacheln aus Isfahan hat er ein Badezimmer wie aus »Tausend und einer Nacht« geschaffen.*

RIGHT: *The artist's work table looks very similar to one of his own still lives.*

FOLLOWING PAGES: *Cees loves colours and his passion for orange, cobalt blue and saffron yellow is evident in the textiles, tiles, Indian scarves and porcelain he has brought back from the Far East. He came back from Isfahan with tons of tiles, with which he created his supremely exotic bathroom.*

A DROITE: *La table de travail de l'artiste ressemble fort à l'une de ses natures mortes.*

DOUBLE PAGE SUIVANTE: *Cees adore la couleur et son goût pour l'orange, le bleu cobalt et le jaune safran se reflète dans les tissus, les carrelages, les châles indiens et les porcelaines dénichés en Extrême-Orient. Il a rapporté un grand nombre de carreaux en faïence de son voyage à Ispahan. La salle de bains semble sortie tout droit des «Mille et Une Nuits».*

HET DIJKHUISJE
Ursula en Edgard Beckand

Noord-Brabant

Vom Deich aus gesehen hat es den Anschein, als verberge sich das Haus von Ursula und Edgard Beckand vor neugierigen Blicken. Doch dieser Eindruck trügt, denn tatsächlich schützt sich dieses Haus am Deich, genau wie all die anderen hübschen »Dijkhuisjes« nur vor dem drohenden Hochwasser, das seit Jahrhunderten wie ein Damoklesschwert über dem flachen Land schwebt. Das niedrige alte Bauernhaus steht nur wenige Meter von der Maas entfernt und ist von einem großen Garten und einigen Nebengebäuden umgeben. Ursula Beckand, einer auf Volkskunst und antike Puppen spezialisierten Antiquitätenhändlerin, und ihrem Mann Edgard, einem Musiker, gefiel das Haus auf Anhieb. Beide begeistern sich für das Landleben und beschlossen, ein idyllisches Heim zu schaffen, das ihre umfangreiche Sammlung von bemalten Möbeln, Raritäten, naiver Kunst und alter Fayence vor dem Hintergrund fröhlicher lebhafter Farben gut zur Geltung bringt. Als neugierige Weltenbummlerin, die sich für jegliche Art von Volkskunst interessiert, hat Ursula aus Europa und Amerika Matten aus bemaltem Tuch, Kelims, Kerzenständer und Vogelkäfige mitgebracht. Und so hat sich ihr ursprünglich typisch holländisches Interieur um Schätze aus aller Welt erweitert.

LINKS: *Ursulas Sammlung von Vogelkäfigen befindet sich unter dem Dach der ehemaligen Scheune.*
OBEN: *Dieses Vogelhäuschen ist ein genaues Abbild der traditionellen Landhäuser in Neuengland.*

LEFT: *Ursula's collection of bird cages, under the eaves of the old barn.*
ABOVE: *This birdcage is a miniature replica of a traditional New England country house.*

A GAUCHE: *La collection de cages à oiseaux d'Ursula a trouvé un abri sous l'auvent de l'ancienne grange.*
CI-DESSUS: *Ce couvoir a la forme exacte d'une maison de campagne traditionnelle de la Nouvelle-Angleterre.*

Ein Meer von Geranien schafft einen bunten Blickfang vor dem Küchenfenster.

A cascade of geraniums makes a splash of brilliant colour by the kitchen window.

Une cascade de géraniums en pot pose une tache de couleur éclatante devant la fenêtre de la cuisine.

When you observe it from the crest of the dyke, you have a distinct impression that the house in which Ursula and Edgard Beckand live is trying to hide away from prying eyes. Not so: like all the other "Dijkhuisjes" in the vicinity, its chief concern for many centuries has been to stay above the floodwaters which have threatened the Netherlands for so many centuries past. The building, a low farmhouse surrounded by a large garden and numerous outbuildings, stands fairly close to the Meuse. Ursula Beckand, an antique dealer with a passion for folk art and antique dolls, and her musician husband Edgard, fell in love with it at first sight. Both have a deep affinity with the countryside, and they decided to put together an idyllic décor using a palette of bright colours that would complete their fine collection of painted furniture, rare objects, naive art and old earthenware. Ursula is a great traveller and a woman of insatiable curiosity about everything to do with folk art. She has brought painted canvas mats, kilims, chandeliers and birdcages home from her travels all over Europe and the Americas, enlivening her otherwise typically Dutch interior with treasures from every corner of the world.

Quand on l'observe du haut de la digue, on a l'impression que la maison d'Ursula et Edgard Beckand essaye de se dérober au regard des curieux. Rien n'est moins vrai, car comme toutes les autres «Dijkhuisjes» rangées en bordure de la digue, elle essaye simplement de se protéger contre l'agression de la crue, cette menaçante épée de Damoclès qui plane depuis des siècles au-dessus du plat pays. Bâtie à deux pas de la Meuse, l'ancienne ferme basse, entourée d'un grand jardin et de plusieurs dépendances, avait tout pour plaire à cette antiquaire passionnée d'art folklorique et de poupées anciennes et à son époux musicien. Comme ils sont sensibles aux charmes de la vie pastorale, ils décidèrent de se construire un décor idyllique composé d'une palette de couleurs gaies et vives qui mettraient en valeur leur belle collection de meubles peints, d'objets rares, de tableaux naïfs et de faïences anciennes. Grande voyageuse et surtout très curieuse de tout se qui touche à l'art folklorique, Ursula a ramené des autres pays d'Europe – et d'Amérique – des tapis en toile peinte, des kilims, des chandeliers et des cages à oiseaux. Son intérieur typiquement hollandais s'est ainsi enrichi d'une multitude de trésors issus des quatre coins du monde.

Das Haus der Beckands schmiegt sich eng an den Deich, als wolle es sich so vor Überschwemmungen schützen.

The Beckands' "dijkhuisje" huddles against the dyke as if it were deliberately sheltering from the danger of flooding.

La maison des Beckand se blottit contre la digue comme si elle cherchait à se protéger des inondations.

In bester Landhaustradition schwören Ursula und Edgard auf kräftige Farben. Das »naive« Porträt aus dem frühen 19. Jahrhundert über dem Kamin stammt aus Neuengland.

Ursula and Edgard favour straightforward colours in the best rural tradition. The portrait over the mantel is an early 19th-century naive work from New England.

Ursula et Edgard adorent les couleurs franches dans la meilleure tradition campagnarde. Le portrait qui trône au-dessus de la cheminée est un naïf du début du 19ᵉ siècle, originaire de la Nouvelle-Angleterre.

OBEN: *Das Juwel der Essecke ist ein Vitrinenschränkchen des 19. Jahrhunderts aus dem Ort Staphorst.*
RECHTS: *Der Kelim-Bezug der Fußstütze passt zum Schablonenmuster des Teppichs aus New Jersey.*
RECHTE SEITE: *In der Küche zeigt der holländische Eckschrank sein blaues Innenleben. An den Türen hat die Hausherrin so genannte »Merklappen« befestigt, die junge Mädchen früher stickten, um den Umgang mit Nadel und Faden zu üben.*

FOLGENDE DOPPELSEITE: *Gelb und Blau sind die Hauptfarben der einladenden Küche. Ein »Merklap« ziert eine der Türen des Eckschranks.*

ABOVE: *The star feature of the dining area is a 19th-century glass-fronted cabinet from Staphorst.*
RIGHT: *The footrest covered in an old kilim fabric blends well with the stencilled New England carpet.*
FACING PAGE: *In the kitchen, the Dutch corner cupboard is painted blue on the inside. Ursula has hung the doors*

with pieces of traditional embroidery – known as "merklappen" – which used to be made by Dutch girls to prove their prowess with needle and silk.
FOLLOWING PAGES: *Exuberant yellows and blues predominate in the kitchen. A "merklap" adorns one of the corner-cupboard's doors.*

CI-DESSUS: *La pièce de résistance du coin-repas est une armoire vitrée 19ᵉ provenant du village de Staphorst.*
A DROITE: *Le repose-pied recouvert d'un kilim ancien se fond dans le décor du tapis peint*

au pochoir, trouvé dans le New Jersey.
PAGE DE DROITE: *Dans la cuisine, l'encoignure hollandaise 19ᵉ offre le beau spectacle de son intérieur peint en bleu pétrole. Sur les battants, Ursula a accroché des broderies traditionnelles – des «merklappen» – que les jeunes filles réalisaient pour prouver leur habilité aux travaux d'aiguille.*
DOUBLE PAGE SUIVANTE: *Le jaune et le bleu dominent la palette exubérante de la cuisine. Un «merklap» orne un des battants de l'encoignure.*

DANKSAGUNG

ACKNOWLEDGEMENTS

REMERCIEMENTS

Es versteht sich von selbst, dass Holland in unseren Herzen einen ganz besonderen Platz einnimmt. Und doch hat unsere Arbeit an diesem faszinierenden Band, für den wir alle Ecken und Winkel der Niederlande bereist haben, unsere Zuneigung für das »flache Land« und seine außergewöhnliche Schönheit noch verstärkt. Die Liste derjenigen, die uns ihr absolutes Vertrauen und ihre Freundschaft geschenkt und damit dieses Buch ermöglicht haben, ist so lang, dass es uns kaum möglich erscheint, alle angemessen zu berücksichtigen. Dennoch möchten wir die Unterstützung von Louise van Everdingen und Claes Conijn besonders hervorheben und uns natürlich auch bei dem Team des Taschen Verlags bedanken, das sich wie immer mit Leib und Seele in das Projekt gestürzt hat.

It goes without saying that Holland occupies a special place in our hearts. Our travels through the length and breadth of the Dutch countryside compiling material for this book have, if anything, increased our affection and appreciation for the beauty of our native land. To thank every individual who gave us wholehearted trust, friendship and assistance in the course of our work would be quite impossible, for the list is quite literally endless. Nevertheless, we cannot omit to mention the steady support afforded us by Mrs. Louise van Everdingen and Mr. Claes Conijn and by the Taschen team, who as usual have done their utmost to ensure the success of this project.

Il va de soi que la Hollande occupe une place prééminente et tout à fait particulière dans nos cœurs. Mais le fait de travailler sur le sujet fascinant du présent ouvrage – et de traverser les Pays-Bas de haut en bas et de long en large –, n'a fait qu'augmenter notre affection pour le «plat pays» et sa beauté remarquable. Remercier tous ceux qui nous ont témoigné leur confiance absolue, qui nous ont fait cadeau de leur amitié et qui nous ont aidés à réaliser cet ouvrage nous paraît impossible tant la liste en est longue. Toutefois, nous ne pouvons omettre de mentionner le support inconditionnel de Madame Louise van Everdingen et de Monsieur Claes Conijn et de toute l'équipe des éditions Taschen qui, comme à l'accoutumée, s'est lancée corps et âme dans la réalisation de ce projet.

Barbara & René Stoeltie

Ambrosius Bosschaert, Blumen in der Vase (1606): Kann man dem Charme dieser üppigen Tulpen, Rosen, Nelken, Iris, Lilien und Papageientulpen tatsächlich widerstehen?

Ambrosius Bosschaert, Flowers in a Glass (1606): A profusion of tulips, roses, carnations, irises, lilies and parrot-tulips to charme the eye.

Ambrosius Bosschaert, Fleurs dans un vase (1606): Comment résister au charme de cette accumulation somptueuse de tulipes, de roses, d'œillets, d'iris, de lys et de tulipes-perroquets?

© 2000 TASCHEN GmbH
Hohenzollernring 53, D-50672 Köln
www.taschen.com
© AKG, Berlin, for the photo on pages 6–7
© Courtesy to the National Gallery of Ireland, Dublin, for the photo on page 32
© National Gallery, London, for the photo on page 10
© Staatliche Kunstsammlungen Dresden Gemäldegalerie Alte Meister,
photo: Klut/Dresden, for the photo on page 28

Design by Catinka Keul, Cologne
Layout by Angelika Taschen, Cologne
Texts edited by Susanne Klinkhamels, Cologne
Lithography by Horst Neuzner, Cologne
English translation by Anthony Roberts, Lupiac
German translation by Marion Valentin, Cologne

Printed in Italy
ISBN 3-8228-0833-4 (edition with German cover)
ISBN 3-8228-6311-4 (edition with English cover)
ISBN 3-8228-6158-8 (edition with French cover)